THERE'S A WAR GOING ON IN MY BACKYARD

Meditations for Gardeners on the Spiritual Life

Douglas G. Scott

RAGGED EDGE PRESS

This Ragged Edge Press publication
was printed by
Beidel Printing House, Inc.
63 West Burd Street
Shippensburg, PA 17257-0152 USA

In respect for the scholarship contained herein, the acid-free paper used in this book meets the guidelines for permanence and durability of the Committee on Production Guidelines for Book Longevity of the Council on Library Resources.

For a complete list of available publications
please write
Ragged Edge Press
Division of White Mane Publishing Company, Inc.
P.O. Box 152
Shippensburg, PA 17257-0152 USA

Library of Congress Cataloging-in-Publication Data

Scott, Douglas, 1949-
    There's a war going on in my backyard : meditations for gardeners
on the spiritual life / Douglas G. Scott.
        p.   cm.
    ISBN 1-57249-114-0 (alk. paper)
    1. Gardeners--Religious life--Meditations.   2. Gardens--Religious
aspects--Christianity--Meditations.   3. Spiritual life--Episcopal
Church--Meditations.   I. Title.
BV4596.G36S37   1998
242'.6--dc21   98-11285
                                                                  CIP

PRINTED IN THE UNITED STATES OF AMERICA

for Jane

TABLE OF CONTENTS

INTRODUCTION viii

ONE
The Gospel in My Garden 1

TWO
There's a War Going On in My Backyard 4

THREE
The Roots of Spirituality 9

FOUR
There's an Azalea in My Plum Tomatoes 13

FIVE
Creature of Earth, Creature of Air 18

SIX
The Surprise That Comes When Confidence Mounts 21

SEVEN
My Companions in the Garden 24

EIGHT
In Season and Out of Season 27

NINE
There's a Hammock in My Garden Where I Think
About My Death 32

TEN
The Gardener Isn't God 35

ELEVEN
Christianity and the Wonderful Weed 39

TWELVE
Some Days My Garden Smells Like Poop 43

THIRTEEN
On Felling a Tree 46

FOURTEEN
Seeds of Change 52

FIFTEEN
     Planting Things I Never Eat 57
SIXTEEN
     A Tale of Two Tomatoes.. 64
SEVENTEEN
     What to Do When Winter Comes.. 68
EIGHTEEN
     Longing for an Orchard.. 73
NINETEEN
     In the Shadow of the Dragon 80
TWENTY
     Starting All Over Again 84

 FOREWORD

The trouble with this book is that it is hard to put down. The style of writing grips the reader.

There is humor in the book—I found myself chuckling from time to time.

There is theological insight in the book. As I hold that theology is the queen of sciences, I welcome that.

Humor and theology, however, cannot by themselves bring me spiritual life. I need a religion which is deeply personal and at the same time, worldwide in its visionary outreach; a religion which makes demands on my will as well as the assent of my intellect.

Douglas Scott gives Christian teaching in a form that is palatable to the reader who is prepared not to gulp, but to chew. I wish it well.

Donald Coggan
101st Archbishop of Canterbury

 ## ACKNOWLEDGMENTS

Everyone who ever gave me a slip of Lily of the Valley or a clump of Hostas or a few spindly orphans from the phlox in their garden helped me to write this book. To those who passed on strawberries or bee balm or Stella D'Oro lilies I extend my deepest gratitude for aiding this work in me. To Saint Martin's Church, who gave me my first good garden, I pledge my gratitude and allegiance.

 INTRODUCTION

In December of 1984, my family and I moved into the rectory of Saint Martin's Church in Radnor, Pennsylvania. Once a carriage house for an old estate, the large stone home seemed cavernous, with a complex tangle of rooms that comes only from architectural evolution. When we arrived with the moving van, our daughters concerned themselves with selecting bedrooms and my wife worried about how we would furnish a living room that measured thirty feet by forty feet. I moved from window to window, looking at the vast expanse of property that surrounded the house. Rather than sitting on one of the web-like suburban roads in the neighborhood, the rectory was placed inside the boundaries of Saint Martin's ten-acre campus. The setting seemed idyllic—stately fieldstone buildings set on manicured lawns, bisected by a stream large enough to be picturesque but not big enough to pose the threat of danger to children. Our new home seemed like an island refuge, set in the midst of an ideal garden.

Garden. Like a spark from an electrical outlet, the word brought a shocking anxiety. Garden. There must be an acre and a half around the house, I thought. I stepped outside and took a quick survey of the property surrounding my new home.

Like a character in a horror movie that is zoomed into his worst nightmare, I realized that at least 140 yards of arbor vitae surrounded the house. A tenacious hedge that grows faster than a three-year old's feet and requires constant trimming and vigilance throughout spring and summer months, it often becomes the permanent home of dreaded mulberry trees at the top and the "poisons" (ivy, oak, and sumac) at its prickly base.

I began counting deciduous trees: a magnificent 35-foot sugar maple, a stately old elm topping 25 feet and two Japanese maples in front. A holly, golden chain, pear, apple, two dogwoods and a magnolia on the side. Three oaks, two flowering cherries, and a few unidentifiable somethings around back. Another dogwood, a birch, and a sickly old tulip poplar by the drive.

I did a few quick mental calculations, and stood rooted to the ground overwhelmed by despair—at least 250 bags of leaves per year. Shredded, at that.

I walked around my new home to the side yard, the only truly private space by the house. While I had glanced at the lay of the yard during my frantic tree count, I did not realize until I stood on the flagstone patio that while the yard retained the basic outline of garden space, it had been a long while since anyone put any time into it. There was no evidence of cultivation — just withered vegetation that had been cut (bearing only marginal resemblance to grass) and vegetation that hadn't been cut (what lazy lawn cutters refer to as "natural areas"). Shivering more from the prospect of what lay ahead than the unseasonably mild December morning, I thrust my hands into my pockets.

"Bet you can't wait to start digging!" The voice behind me bellowed with a cheeriness suggesting that the bearer was chronically immune to the pain of others. I turned to see a member of the church's vestry walking toward me. We had met during the interview process, but I was having a difficult time remembering his name. "You know," he said, pulling out a pipe and filling it with shag from an old vinyl pouch, "one of the reasons we picked you was that you put down 'gardening' as a hobby in your résumé. We figured there would be plenty here to keep you busy!"

I gave him the earnest look of a convicted man who begs his attorney to explain the jury's verdict. "How much yard work does the vestry expect me to do?" I asked.

He knit his eyebrows in apparent confusion while digging deep into his pockets for a light. "Well," he said, finding a kitchen match and cutting it into flame with a thumbnail, "I suppose as much as it takes!"

We stood in silence for a few minutes. I was struggling to understand what he meant by "as much as it takes," while he puffed luxuriantly, no doubt envisioning the Eden that was about to emerge. "After all," he exclaimed, "you're the gardener!" He patted me on the shoulder and took his leave, offering a few words of welcome and the promise of a dinner at his wife's table "somewhere down the line."

I was the gardener. True enough, I had put 'gardening' on my *Curriculum Vitae* as a pastime, but I was referring to a small square of New Jersey soil in a previous parish that was so rich it would have grown dollar bushes if I had planted pennies. I had tomatoes (*everybody* in New Jersey has tomatoes) and peppers to fry with Italian sweet sausage and eggplant to slice, bread and fry into chips. There were some beans and snap peas with a marigold border to keep away the bugs. That and a disastrous attempt at raspberries which made me a frequent customer at the local emergency ward was the sum of my gardening experience.

They thought they had hired the reincarnation of Jim Crockett, but I was only Jack of bean stalk fame.

We are all gardeners. We all tend some patch of space or time or activity. We invest effort and energy, we contend against forces beyond our control which threaten the security or fruitfulness of our garden spaces, we long for a product to which we can point with pride, allowing satisfaction to spread within our hearts. Ultimately, we become the garden we tend, allowing the lines between garden and gardener to dissolve, encouraging in ourselves and others the association of work with the worker.

In the thirteen years since I stood shrouded in worry in my new back yard, I have made astonishing discoveries about myself as a human being and child of God, a father and husband and as a priest. Much of what I have learned was forged in the garden I tend, working both the soil and the spirit. This book is a record of those discoveries.

Having said that, I must admit to some discomfort with the project. "Spirituality" is a hot topic in the latter half of our decade. Bookshelves, magazines and the media are filled with advice on how to access the spiritual side of human nature. The remarkable popularity of these writings seems to suggest a hunger on the part of many people in our society to reclaim something lost, to rectify the emptiness of our consumer-oriented culture. Much of the material being published is characterized by a "how-to" flavor, as though living spiritually was akin to making furniture at home or weaving wreaths for your front door from local wild vines. Other books and articles focus on spirituality in the self-help vein, characterized, I believe, by our willing embrace of the insufficiency of the self, insisting that before progress is to be made one must admit to a lack of development or a state of personal or emotional inadequacy. Still others, perhaps most tragically, depend on the embrace of an attitude of dualism, that is, of the intellectual assertion to the notion that there are two levels of reality, one physical, another spiritual. Because of the mutually exclusive nature of these two realms, one must leave one in order to participate fully in the other. Many of these works insist that valid spirituality is evidenced by extraordinary behavior or unusual physical manifestations.

I fear that most of these approaches are desperately flawed, and that in fact many of them are simply opportunistic. In the same way that misguided men and women have always come forward with bogus remedies for real problems, the overwhelming majority of writers churning out spiritual solutions for human emptiness provide little relief for personal pain and human despair. "Breathe this way, repeat this mantra, retreat into self," many current practitioners proclaim, imposing difficult, almost unachievable prescriptions for those who long to find their way to wholeness. While there is much to be said for measured, focused breathing and serious self-examination, the fact is that spirituality is not achieved through mechanized ends, nor can it be realized through detachment from the environment in which we live.

Simply stated, spirituality is not a goal, nor is it to be found in another 'place' or dimension—it is a vital part of our humanity, decidedly incarnational. Living spiritually does not depend on the acquisition of some set of skills or secret actions. It is as close as our own muscle tissue, as much a part of us as our breath. In fact, living spiritually is quite simple and always more near to us than we imagine. Rather than being in a state of enlightenment achieved by separation from our lives, it is in life itself—in our work, in our homes, in our relationships with family, friends, and strangers. Spirituality is, in fact, the fabric which holds all these disparate parts of life together, the web of connection which gives shape and substance to human living. But like garden space long unused, we frequently neglect our spirits, allowing the richness of the human spirit to lay fallow, leeched of its power and vitality.

Reclaiming the treasure of human spirituality, like reclaiming a garden long ignored, requires some simple but often strenuous work. It may not (in fact, most often *does not*) manifest itself in bizarre or abnormal behaviors, but is rather evidenced by fruit which is entirely consistent with the seeds planted in the human heart. Perhaps most important, the ability of the individual to be open to and directed by the Spirit of God depends not on what we do, but rather on what we allow God to do in us. For the garden of God is not found in some distant or hidden dimension, but in the daily lives of men and women. We are the garden, and the eternal desire of the Holy One is that we might allow God to work the soil of the human spirit well and become God's pleasant planting.

ONE

The Gospel in My Garden

As a gardener, I'm grateful that I know my Bible. As a Bible student, I'm grateful that I garden.

Jesus was a gardener. I'm convinced of it. He may have been trained as a carpenter, but had he not been the Messiah of God, I believe he would have farmed the land for a living. This is a fairly strong claim, and no doubt there are many Biblical scholars who would challenge this conclusion. But as anyone who reads their Bible can tell, Jesus knew the land. He knew about planting and seasons and crops and the problems of gardeners. Some might say that Jesus chose the stories he told because of his familiarity with his audience, but in all his teaching, he displays an authoritative grasp of the problems and techniques of farming. He demonstrates a command of the work that goes well beyond information, exhibiting a mastery that is grounded in experience.

He never speaks of carpentry, never shares a parable based on the idiosyncracies of wood or the use of the woodsmith's tools. In all his teaching, he never speaks of grain or board, axe or blade. He speaks of two builders at one point, but the pivotal point of the story is not the skill of the builder, but the builder's knowledge of the land and its suitability as a foundation for what is to be built. Yet many of our romantic notions of Jesus are grounded in our image of "the carpenter from Nazareth," our hymns celebrating the one whose "hands were skilled at the plane and the lathe." Don't believe it. Jesus was a gardener.

In the Gospel, Jesus speaks of so many things that happen to me as a gardener. But if I were a gardener alone, without being a Christian, I would think of these events as nothing more than difficulties that come with the task of planting, never seeing that the work in my garden mirrors the greater events of life itself. The more I study, the more I plant, the more I am certain—the garden and its attendant work are a microcosm of earthly existence. In its tasks are found a model of all of life's work. In the symbiotic interrelatedness of plant and soil, there exists an archetype of our

1

relatedness to each other and to God. In the garden there is understanding to be found—understanding of Jesus, of Jesus' mind, of Jesus' heart.

I am up to my arms in tangled, scaly growth, trying to sort out one strand from another, anxious to prune the secondary but not the primary stalks. Working the grape arbor next to my house is like trying to untangle a knotted ball of string. But unlike string, which can be discarded if it can't be sorted out, there is an urgency to this work. If the vine is pruned incorrectly, I forfeit this year's growth. Grasping shears, my hands enter the tangled web, following one branch, looking for the nodes of new growth. I make a cut and feel the satisfying dry crunch of a dead stalk between the blades of my cutter. I trace another, and am now so caught in the web of a branch that it surrounds me. I cut again but feel resistance in the blade and know I have erred. I have cut a living branch and as soon as I slice through the pith, it bleeds. The branch actually bleeds, soaking my hand in sap which rushes freely from the point of incision. Here, half a dozen yards from the root, the branch pumps out its life into my hands. "I am the vine," Jesus says, "you are the branches." The words come to me as a shocking intrusion into the task. This grape arbor isn't just a place to sweat and toil—it is a mirror of my connection to this Jesus, and no matter how distant that Jesus may seem at times, his blood pumps through my veins. The useless parts of me, the extraneous dead parts need to be discarded, cut ruthlessly away if I am to remain rooted to the vine.

I am spent. It has taken three hours to complete the major seed planting in the late spring of the year. Seedlings won't go in the ground for another week, perhaps two, but the things I grow from seed—radishes, carrots, squash, beans, pumpkins, watermelon—have just been set in their spaces. I scooped mounds of soil spaced carefully apart from one another, or made even furrows in the ground, covering the tiny seeds with a fine blanket of soil. Now I sit exhausted on my patio, feeling guilty that there are still seeds in packets beside me which will never be planted. When I can gather the strength, I go inside to shower, and after I am washed and refreshed I look out the window only to see the sparrows and crows and jays working the mounds and furrows I have just planted, certain that there are treasures to be found. I rush out to shoo them away, knowing that I can't keep the birds out of my garden forever. They will return as soon as I have gone, acting out an eternal dance destined to reduce the number of pumpkin pies in my larder this fall. "A sower went out to sow some seed," Jesus says, "and some was thrown on the wayside, some eaten by the birds . . ." Not everything that I do lasts—not in my garden, not in my family, not in my work. Sometimes my best effort, my hardest work, is futile. At times it is undermined by others or by my own inner conflict, sometimes things just don't work out. I imagine God feels much the same way about me. Not everything God intends for me works out. Sometimes my own greed or worry or willfulness prevents God from bringing to full growth that which

God has planted in me. Not everyone understands this. It helps to watch the birds in your garden eating the seed you have just planted.

I am constantly amazed that the tiniest seeds produce such lavish growth. Seeds no bigger than a pencil point, ones which I have a hard time handling because they are so small—these have so much power in them that left to their own devices in a warm, wet place, they will explode into something that has the ability to add excitement to my table and nourishment to my body. "Look at the mustard seed," Jesus says. "If you only had that much faith, you could move mountains." Since I am unable to move mountains, it's humbling to think that my faith is even less than the tiny pin dots I hold in my hand before the planting. Not my believing—my believing is huge. We give intellectual assent, belief, to lots of things we don't have faith in. Our faith is what we do about our beliefs. If the truth were told, I profess sound believing in the goodness of God, but I often act as though I believed only in me.

It's a miracle. A week after my planting, lots of little green things are breaking through the surface of the soil. Despite the birds and the sudden cold snap and the tininess of the seed, there are living things pushing their heads above the soil. I am amazed. I have done so little. Nature has done so much. Jesus said, "A man plants some seed and goes to bed. Days later, the seed is grown, he knows not how." God gives the growth, but I have had a hand in it. Without my willingness to plant, the garden would not exist. "Without God, we cannot," Saint Augustine wrote, "Without us, God will not."

The apple tree in the far corner of the yard has stood for at least 50 years. Each year apples are set but the fruit is misshapen, withered, bitter to the taste. I fertilize, prune, worry about the tree and keep hoping that fruit will yet come. I save seeds from the fallen fruit in hopes that I can grow new seedlings to replace the tree itself. Finally, I call in the famous county extension agent the gardening books all speak about. He walks around the tree, slices into a branch, and heads off. "Bad tree," he says tersely. "Cut it down." Jesus echoes his diagnosis. "Only a good tree can bear good fruit. Bad trees produce bad fruit. You can tell what kind of tree it is by the fruit it produces." The tree comes down, the birds splash in a basin I place upon the stump, the apple wood hisses in my woodstove later in the year, and I wonder what fruit others see in me.

The parable of the wicked tenants, the parable of the laborers in the vineyard, the teaching about the seasons of the year, the parable of the tares and the wheat—over and over, Jesus returns to the garden to uncover the greatest truths about the kingdom. And I stand in my garden, surrounded by so many kingdom-signs, grateful for the work which allows me to uncover them all.

TWO

There's a War Going On in My Backyard

Once upon a time I believed the naive voices of my age which urged me to embrace the wisdom of nature's harmony. I thought of the earth as a benevolent and evolving system of mutuality, where earth and seed, water and sky all interacted to produce the highest good for itself. The earth was a peaceful place and, left undisturbed, would fulfill its destiny for gentle richness. Human activity, I was persuaded, introduced the only negative element in the unfolding of earthly bounty. We destroyed, interrupted, interfered, raped, mutilated. What was once virgin land unbounded in its potential for productivity had become a collection of parking lots. Gentle downs and pristine meadows forever disappeared in favor of strip malls and hamburger drive-ins. This was the human legacy in a once verdant and bountiful land. By the very nature of my genus, I was a perpetrator, my guilt shared with those generations who longed to air condition creation.

Return to simple ways, my culture cries. Embrace the mind and heart of the native who killed only what she ate and saw the soil beneath her feet as a blood relative. Better yet, find your path in the life of the wolf and the otter, the deer and the beaver, which live in the world without diminishing the environment. Leave the earth as you found it, unsullied by human touch. Wear natural fibers, recycle your refuse, bike or walk rather than drive.

"All these I have obeyed from my youth," I want to say as did the rich young man who begged Jesus for the secret to eternal life. And I believed it all, embracing the party line of the age of ecology, until I looked at my backyard.

Two months of work in my long neglected little yard convinced me that my world view was desperately skewed. The truth is that nature is aggressive, violent, capricious, and chaotic. I learned this from the war going on in my backyard.

The battlefield which extends beyond my patio (the closest thing to a neutral zone I have) sports every tactical asset prized by military commanders. There are extensive ground troops in my battle zone, present in

4

an astonishing array of battalions as different from one another as the dog soldiers of the infantry are from elite Special Forces units. Ants amass unseen forces in subterranean installations more carefully hidden than Saddam Hussein's nuclear research facilities. Slugs, like Gideon's raiders, slink through the cover of darkness to wreck destruction only on the most expensive cultivated produce. Spiders by the hundreds of thousands whose sheer numbers, like the fierce highland warriors of Scotland, leave the single human trying to lay claim to a small piece of dirt feeling helpless and overpowered. Leggy things move with the lightning speed of forward regiments, boasting remarkable tenacity. Try to brush them off a forearm or the back of your neck and these centipedes and millipedes and earwigs display an astonishing adhesiveness meant to intimidate even the most intrepid warrior. Other bugs. Lots of other bugs. Bugs whose names I don't know, and with whom I have no desire to be intimate. Bugs who appear just as I lovingly scoop the soil to make room for a primrose. Bugs whose very appearance is as daunting as angry Celts who wore the woad.

Rommel had his Panzers and Patton his Shermans, and benevolent nature have its armored divisions in my backyard. Moles and voles and mice and bunnies and rats and squirrels whose defense comes not from metal plate but from the affectionate memories of the gardener himself, raised with tender tales by Beatrix Potter and Kenneth Grahame and Roald Dahl. Unlike their storybook counterparts, these voracious troopers run riot above and below ground, with such efficient forays into the lands of pampered leaf and emerging fruit that there is little doubt about the reality and efficacy of cross-species intelligence gathering.

The air forces of nature are far more imposing and effective than all the Phantoms and Eagles and Hawkeyes at the disposal of the modern fighter pilot, for the greatest dangers to the human in the garden are the things that fly. It was nature's air force that first led me to question the much touted benevolence of nature. Divebombing flies and stealth mosquitos, invisible midges and swarming gnats: what earthly purpose do they serve beyond the repulsion of the adversary from the theater of war? Bees may produce earth's sweetest nectar, but what value is the yellow jacket? Is it possible that the yellow jacket is simply nature's revenge for the steel and glass intrusions of humankind into the cloudless sky?

These are the troops waging war in my backyard—nature's army and air forces, with animate allies too gruesome to examine or describe. But these are not nature's principal weapons. The most powerful, most destructive ordnance in earth's arsenal, like human troops, is colored green.

The first salvo to make itself felt in my garden was the tenacious morning glory. As a child, I loved their sunny striped blossoms which greeted morning's first rays. If I felt some sadness for the brevity of the fragile flowers' one-day lifespan, I rejoiced that there were always more buds the next morning to take the place of the withered blooms of yesterday. Like faithful soldiers who would drop their Enfields to grasp our nation's flag when the banner bearer fell, the morning glory seemed inexhaustible in its ability to display what beauty it had to offer the rising sun.

When I cleared the first beds for flowers in the garden at Saint Martin's rectory, I happily pulled out weeds with expectant abandon, thinking only of the marigolds and snapdragons and zinnias which would take their place. In my innocence, I believed that my garden hungered for the effort I lavished upon it, that it would mold itself to my vision for a place of ordered beauty. I soon found that the morning glory was more than just a vining plant. It was nature's resistance movement, more fierce, more resourceful than Polish freedom fighters or World War II French saboteurs. With silphen threads of green, the morning glories wound around my verbena, saturated my impatiens. I hadn't expected my garden to be weed free, but I was unprepared for the ferocity of nature's resistance to my efforts to keep it so. I looked with alarm at the $250 worth of seedlings which punctuated my weed patch. With sinking heart, I realized the worst—pull the weed and you kill the seedling.

Like a blind man who sees for the first time, like the deaf whose ears are unstopped, I saw my garden for what it truly was—an arena in which the riotous struggle for survival is played out. Plants stretch beyond their anchoring dirt to escape the shade of the trees whose roots sponged the moisture from the surrounding ground, which was clogged with the chickweed squeezing out the grass, which formed the thatch, which sucked the dew leaving the turf hard as dried cake. I saw with new eyes that branch is sword and vine is whip and leaves are spoiled children who shove and elbow and push siblings aside in order to bask in the warmth of generous light. Young shoots strain upwards, starting from scratch when tender stalk is broken by passing fox or heel of dog.

With my fingers still trying to sort out glory vine from scabiosa I saw this little world around me pushing, straining, moving with sun, reaching for rain, its desperate stretch toward life not to be denied. There was no harmony here, no indwelling mutuality or romantic notion of filial connection. Here in this little plot the struggle for life raged and screamed in slow but certain motion. Like writhing serpents exploding from Medusa's scalp, the green things around me swayed with serpentine single-mindedness toward sunlight, air, moisture. I was no savior, I who thought to bring order to this little space—I was the intruder, the pretender who sought to impose my vision on willful land. The natives of this land would struggle against me and ultimately succeed, for I would deploy what meager forces I command only for a time, then I would be gone.

Crosses and cairns mark the failure of the vanquished on the world's battlefields; so too stood the specters of the failure of those who had lost the battle here before me. Here was a scrubby thing that had once been an Easter azalea, perhaps given in love and planted in hope, now reduced to a spray of upturned sticks and a smattering of leaves, denied the acidic soil it craves in order to blossom and grow. Here, no higher than my furthest reach, an elderly maple tree with two dead limbs and a hollowed trunk. Over there a clump of strand-like leaves that once sported a velvety purple iris. A concrete bird bath so heavy that I cannot lift the basin, but nonetheless toppled by a deceptively tenacious web of wild grapevine. Others had come here and failed, as I must fail. They enjoyed their labors for a while, perhaps adorning their table with the iris arranged in a bud vase next to a warm crusty pie made from a handful of apples. But in the end, the battle was won by the very force which I now seek to tame for a season. I am under no delusions. It will prevail when I am gone to another garden, earthly or heavenly. But for the joy of the work, and perhaps as an act of faith, I press my spade into the earth once again and demand that nature yield.

But wait! I damn the aggressive single-mindedness of the earth as though it were something outside of self, something other than what I am, but are we that different, my garden and I? If nature is the ground of all that runs riot in my backyard, in fact, riot itself, is there not some part of me which longs to be left untamed? Do I not possess a spirit, a soul which resents intrusion by those outside of self who long to shape me, mold me, make me in their own image? Does not the same nature which drives the weed and insect drive me? And doesn't my world insist on compliance with that nature's longing for a lack of outside intervention? From my earliest days, benign men who came into my day within the confines of my television neighborhood told me that they liked me as I was, demanding no change, no growth, not even the inconvenience of relational interactivity. My bookshelves became filled with the pulp which promised that I was OK, as you are OK. I not only live in, but contribute to a century which has abolished the rules, removed the restrictions, touted the freedom which has anchored our fears, promoted our litigiousness, convinced me of my right to conflict with those whom I find different. My body is mine, my home is my castle, my car is my pride. My education transmits information, but does not mold my character, which is satisfactory just the way it is. Human beings are ready to use, we insist. No modification necessary.

But I know that even if everyone else is OK the way they come from the package, I certainly am not. For within myself I feel as tangled and matted and restless as the garden around me. And while I may try to plant the virtues I long for, they, like my tomatoes and eggplant, are constantly under attack by some force I thought I had weeded out a long time before. I am afraid more than an "OK person" should be. I am embarrassed because something about the things I do and say isn't right. I worry. I worry about what I have done and what I am going to do and, for that matter, what I am doing right now. And yes, there are moments of unbounded joy and deep satisfaction and peace which abides for a time. But those moments are punctuated with other, more insidious realities which grab and cling and choke.

I can't be alone in this. There must be others who know that to tend the human spirit is to tend a fertile spot that gives life and space to growing things both good and bad. Further, we must know that there exists a force, a power as ubiquitous as nature itself, which seeks to undo all the good that is done in the plantings of the human heart.

Despite the insistence of the environmental purists, the fact remains that just because nature is what it is doesn't mean that nature is all it might become. There is, after all, a difference between a garden and the wilderness. Without the hand of the gardener (and the tools which the gardener employs) nature is condemned to endless battle. In the same way, the human spirit, left untended, unworked, must remain tangled, conflicted.

So the work begins, in the soil of both home and heart. And like all good work, it begins with a swell of expectation that progress can be made.

THREE
The Roots of Spirituality

Five large spreading yews stand in front of my home. The smallest is six feet tall, the tallest tops eight feet. Each is carefully trimmed to resemble a tall, dark green column of impenetrable growth. Whoever planted them and allowed them to grow so high did so foolishly, because each stands directly in front of a window in the house, either living room or study. They effectively block daylong sunlight from the house, leaving our home as dark as a tomb. While it is true that in the spring we can watch a robin or two construct a nest in the tangle of needle and branch safely behind a window, my family is condemned to darkness by living in the yews' shadows.

Despite my affection for things living, I have decided that light in my home is more important than maintaining the number of spreading yews in the world. While I might miss their stately appearance, I will not miss the miserable red berries which stain everything they touch, nor the comments from friends who try to find our home: "We couldn't see the house for those bushes!" The yews must go.

The first part is easy. Get out the chainsaw, fight my way through the branches like *Ramar of the Jungle*, get to the base and cut. I had considered pulling the bushes out with a chain attached to my truck, but with my luck the roots probably grew under the face of the house and I would be forced to become a remodeler instead of a gardener. Within fifteen minutes all five bushes are down and my wife moves from window to window inside the house, wrapped in streaming shafts of sunshine.

Once the yews are cut into manageable pieces and shredded, destined for compost and mulch, I make the foolish assumption that the stumps should be fairly easy to remove—a few well-placed cuts of major roots, a little sweat, some oomph, and *voilá*—new space for bleeding heart or coreopsis. Unfortunately, reality is always more cruel than imagination.

I have cut every major root I can find, admiring the deep red heart of the wood, but the first trunk sits solidly in the ground. The digging starts, I find a few more major roots, cut them away, pull again. I might as well tie a rope around the Washington Monument and try to drag it off center. Some-where, the yew-gods are laughing. It must be time for more serious tools. Wrecking bar, impact drill with chisel bit, rototiller, reciprocating saw: all the massive implements of labor which give men a false sense of power. Nothing.

It is obvious that there is nothing for it except to dig a wide pit at the farthest possible perimeter, deep enough to find roots like hair instead of roots like steel cable. The work takes fully ten days and the front of my house looks like the impact site of a meteor shower.

"Having a little trouble with the bushes?" a friend asks halfway through the work, no doubt secretly glad that he has not suffered from the shrub-bery mania of former owners.

"Let me tell you," I wheeze, "these yews were *connected*."

Everything is connected to one degree or another. From my spread-ing yews which had a root system equal to its above-the-ground habit to the tiniest seedling which proudly sports an inch-long tap root. The me-dium of their connection is the soil, and while they draw life from the earth around them, they also contribute to its texture and chemical composition. Anyone who has ever tried companion planting knows this. The gardener who plants tomatoes within sight of a black walnut tree is sure to be disap-pointed. Plant those tomatoes next to potatoes and failure is assured, yet intertwined with peppers and eggplant, they thrive. This is a great truth, often ignored: not only do growing things draw life from the medium which supports them, the medium takes on the characteristics of the things which grow in it. This is the significant signpost which leads us to a true under-standing of spirituality.

In our culture, many people are searching for a deeper and more permanent aspect of human life. They desperately want to be spiritual. Many of them look for experience in nonearthly places, longing for "out of body" experiences or mystical departures from the mundanity of everyday living. They might as well search for a left-handed smoke shifter.

It is certainly true that individuals in every time and every culture have spoken of extraordinary mental or emotional experiences. Despite the beau-tiful or frightening nature of these accounts, they all share one thing—they are *disconnected from life*. Whether we read of the revelations granted to Saint Francis or Theresa of Avila or read the current accounts of detached hoverings over an operating table, each mystic or supernatural experience moves above or beyond the plane of human living. I will not deny that many of these accounts are accurate descriptions of some event, but I must insist that this is not spirituality. These experiences are sufficiently rare to indicate to us that they are available to only a gifted few, or to those with delusional tendencies. If this is spirituality, the vast majority of men and women are consigned to living without it.

True spirituality is connectedness with the life force which drives us, not the successful negotiation of some realm beyond our knowing. Like

the yew and the seedling, it is the depth of our "root being" which deter-
mines the richness of our spiritual aspect. Unlike dramatic netherworld
events, true spirituality is not episodic, but constant in its nature. Just as
the tree or plant must be rooted in the ground *all the time* in order to live, so
we must constantly be rooted in something spiritual to survive. The danger, of course, is that we often long to be in some other state, some other
medium, certain that the greatest quest in life is learning how to escape life
itself. There are times in our lives when the events which envelop us seem
so harsh, so worrisome that we become convinced that nothing holy, nothing divine could dwell with us in the chaos of illness or unemployment or
child worry. This time of stress and anxiety is not a product of our culture,
but of our nature. Humans long to escape the devastating immediacy of
distress. In my own times of confusion and uncertainty, I have found a
kindred soul in the author of Psalm 51 who seems to know my desire for
escape:

> The noise of war surrounds me,
> and the horror of battle overwhelms me.
> I said, 'Oh, that I had wings like a dove!
> I would fly away and be at rest.'

Convinced that no good can be derived from the experience of human pain
or distress, we, like the silly soldiers in *Monty Python and the Holy Grail*,
move ever away singing our song of escape: "Run away! Run away!"

But the testimony of scripture and of generations of nonpsychic men
and women is that our rootedness is to be found here—here where we live
and work, here where both the painful and joyous events of life play out,
here in the world that is matter and Spirit entwined.

When his disciples asked for answers to ultimate questions about
God, Jesus didn't lapse into theological discourse, nor did he provide means
for terrestrial escape. Instead, he turned their gaze toward earth itself: Do
you want to understand God, to know about the movement of God's hand?
Look here—at this flower, at that tree, at the field over there. These are
your teachers. If you want to know about heavenly things, you must understand earthly things. That is the path to seek, that is the way.

Like the roots in my garden, life-based spirituality understands that
the medium is affected by the growing things set in it. Most of us assume
that God never changes, but the Bible is filled with stories of how human
activity delights or angers or saddens God. In fact, if we are true to our
tradition of belief, we must admit that God is affected by the actions of men
and women. God is *susceptible* to the character and quality of our lives.
God's interest in us is not casual or detached; we are part and parcel of the
reality of divine life. And, rooted in the Spirit, we affect God. God feels our
pain, rejoices in our pleasure, is wounded by our sin.

Understanding this makes us aware of the incredible consequences
of our spirituality. Just as God carries our joy at the birth of our children and

bears our pain at the death of our parents, so, too, God's action is restricted when subjected to our immobility. One of the most remarkable passages in the New Testament tells of a time when Jesus returns to his home in Galilee, to neighbors and friends who had watched him grow up. Perhaps their familiarity with him increased their incredulity because Saint Matthew tells us, "...he did not do many great works there because of their unbelief." Can it be that Jesus was dependent on those around him for the administration and efficacy of his power? It would seem as though we are dependent on the Spirit for our life, but that God is dependent on us for vitality. Separate one from the other, and both are less.

Our groundedness in the Spirit has even greater consequences. Just as a plant can thrive because of adjacent planting, our spiritual grounding allows us a richness of relationships with all life rooted in the Spirit. I don't know why my tomatoes are affected by the black walnut tree planted 30 feet away. Certainly, their roots don't touch. But through the medium of soil, one clearly affects the other, shapes and conditions the quality and character of its life. Haven't we who pray found this to be true, that the energy and attention we devote to our intercessions and petitions affects the quality of life of those for whom we pray? Can it be that the very Spirit which is the medium of our spirit life is enriched, energized, engorged by the intensity and effort of our praying? Science seems mystified by data that suggests that sick people who are prayed for seem to improve, but is that a mystery to those of us who move purposefully through the medium of God's Spirit to lift up and support those in need? We should not be surprised. Science asks "how?" The "hows" are not readily apparent in the laboratory, but in the garden.

Like the yews in my front yard, tearing someone from the Spirit is a difficult, if not impossible task. Can there be any higher life goal, any deeper desire than to be infused with the Spirit of God at all times and in all places; to find that each new breath, each act of compassion takes us deeper and deeper into the very heart of God? Would anyone leave such an atmosphere willingly? Saint Paul, planted in the Spirit with a wonderful and highly-developed root system, proclaims to early Roman Christians with joy, "For I am convinced that neither death, nor life, nor angels, nor rulers, nor things present, nor things to come, nor powers, nor height, nor depth, nor anything else in all creation, will be able to separate us from the love of God in Christ Jesus our Lord."

No doubt Saint Paul was laughing as I placed perennials in my front yard the following spring. Clearing away the soil to make room for new growth, I found five little yews reaching for heaven.

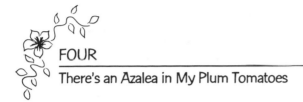

FOUR

There's an Azalea in My Plum Tomatoes

I believe in ghosts. I believe that the spirits of those who have passed to greater life retain their identity, their individuality, and their relationships. I believe that they stand in the nearer presence of God and continue to love us, long for us, and make urgent intercession on our behalf. And because I believe that the earth is God's place and that we live in a unified cosmos, I believo those ghosts are present to us as well; that they surround us with their comfort and care and long for the day when we will join them In that state where there is no pain or grief, but life eternal. My heart and my hope and all the reason I can muster persuades me. I believe in ghosts.

I believe in other kinds of ghosts as well. This belief comes not from hope or heavenly longing, but from hard experience. You see, there are ghosts in my garden. Like the wraiths which move effortlessly between the dimensions of spirit and flesh, the ghosts in my garden move with remarkable facility between the realms of soil and air. These ghosts haunt me, undo me in my attempts to make safe space for growing things.

But unlike the spirits which comprise the communion of the saints, and unlike those which in story and sensational account plague homes, or even those which frighten children at Halloween, these ghosts are far more insidious, more willing to kill and maim. For the ghosts that haunt my garden are grapevine and chickweed, mulberry and Bishopswort. They lie in wait deep below the surface of the earth watching, waiting as I till and feed and plant. Some, like an inexperienced race horse anxious to bolt at the gate, speed upward toward the soil's surface as soon as I have broken ground, eager to show their dominance. But others lie in wait, far wiser than their youthful and anxious cousins. In my mind's eye, I see them watching as the roots of my seedlings reach deeper into the earth, waiting patiently for the moment when they can snake and wind, embrace and entangle themselves effectively in my planting. With a wisdom born of generations of experience and selection, they have, I believe, a knowing which approaches consciousness. Devoid of malice or benevolence, their insight is born out of the same hunger which drives all living things—the need to survive.

I have done all that I think is necessary to make an orderly space in chaotic ground. I have tilled my soil deep, carefully removing each clump of unwanted green, scanning the ground for stray root or seed pod. I raked my garden smooth and level, breaking up the clods of dirt. I made furrows and mounds and planted, watering daily with a gentle spray so as not to dislodge carefully placed seeds or tender young plants. Mounds of mulch protected the base of my precious seedlings. String and stake marked the borders of my garden as a warning to all intruders, human or animal. I might as well have hung out a neon sign: "Weeds Wanted Here."

A month has passed since my planting. I have attacked the early weeds that have bolted from the soil's surface with vigor and vengeance. Most of them came out easily, and I deluded myself into thinking that keeping this space weed free would be a matter of relative ease. But I have just looked closely at the young bush beans which stand no higher than my ankles. Wrapped around each stem I clearly see a double strand of some unidentified vine, its long triangular leaves hiding from view under the leaves of my beans. Frantically, I run to other beds, and find that they are here too—slithering up my tomatoes, entwined around peppers and eggplant.

Jesus tells a story of a farmer who finds that weeds are growing side by side next to his wheat. As I look at the stranglehold which the morning glory has on my planting, I feel a brother to the man. As he looks at his field, he felt the same feeling of defeat I feel and mutters under his breath, "An enemy has done this." I wonder if he believed in ghosts, too.

The garden in which I work has quite a history. As far as I can determine, this land was first worked by a family just before the turn of the eighteenth century. The parish house of Saint Martin's Church, an old estate called Bolingbroke, stands sixty yards away from my home. The oldest piece of that grand old home is a simple stone farmhouse built in the year 1700. Radnor Township, where Bolingbroke is located, was established just eighteen years before the construction of the farmhouse, a large geographical square home to a significant number of farmers. The War for Independence was three-quarters of a century away, and the main line of the Pennsylvania Railroad, from which this area now takes its name, was still in the distant future. The area is perfectly suited to farming—rolling land rich with the loam of generations of deciduous trees, mild winters and a growing season which extends from cool and sunny spring times to crisp autumn seasons separated by a hot and humid summer, running from early June through late September.

I don't know what the cash crop of the first gardener in this place was, although I suspect that like other farms in the area it was likely to be corn or wheat. I like to tell visitors that it is possible that the farm helped supply the encampment at Valley Forge during the deadly winter of 1777, but as the politics of the area (then as now) were decidedly conservative, I suppose it is highly unlikely. I do know that in later years, an apple orchard was a large part of the property, as was a forty-yard grape arbor. One of the apple trees still stands, remarkable for the beauty of its form, the number of bees its blossoms draw in the spring, and the wasps which flock to its fallen fruit. The grapevines on the old iron arbor are now gone, but the birds, nature's most efficient planters, have seen to it that wild grapevine grows everywhere on the property.

When I first moved into the rectory, the garden testified to its more recent history. The side yard, which I now work, contained no less than a dozen balsam trees which were obviously planted by someone who never imagined them fully grown. Now they are bare and straggly, each having lost coveted sun to the other. Spreading yews had really spread, hanging over walkways, dominating their space. The dreaded arbor vitae slunk like a giant boa constrictor through the yard, dividing one reasonably sized space into three spaces too small for recreation, too shaded for flowers or vegetables.

In short, a lot of planting has been done here over the years and the earth which now hosts stock and ghost has, like a dressmaker's mannequin, sported the living handiwork of many a gardener. I feel quite humbled that this same space has yielded to the whims and fancies of so many workers, and that I am only the most recent in a long line of those who have come to dirt expectantly.

Weeding takes up more of my time as the season progresses. The chickweed displays a disconcerting resiliency. Though my garden is cleared in the evening, the morning's first light breaks on the orphaned chicks of the weed I savaged just hours before. But now the work is harder as spring's cool air is replaced by early summer's heat and the soil is salted by my sweat which drops onto the ground. Still, at the close of the day, my little plot looks good, fresh as it did when the land was first tilled.

I lead my wife into the garden with obvious pride and show her the results of my labor. She smiles, comments on the progress I have made, and makes a dutiful tour of the rows of my expectation. "That's a funny looking tomato," she says, no doubt expecting me to expound on the virtues of one of the five varieties I have planted.

"Where?" I ask.

"Over there," she says, pointing to my Roma plums, famous for their thick and fleshy walls, perfect for sauces and purees.

"Oh, the plum tomatoes!" I beam.

"No—there, in the middle of the plum tomatoes."

My brow furrows and I move closer, looking at the odd growth she has spotted. It's not a tomato at all, but rather a small bunch of shoots, uniform in size and height bearing small oval leaves. It isn't a weed, at least not one I have seen before. I wrap my hand around its base and tug gently, so as not to disturb the Romas on either side. More than resistance, I feel a connectedness which indicates that whatever this is, it's deep. Something makes me stop and, squatting on my haunches, I realize what Jane has found.

"This is an azalea," I say out loud.

"Oh, lovely!" Jane exclaims. "I hope it's a pink one!" She walks off, delighted at the prospect of flowering shrubbery.

I move outside the border of my garden, sit on the ground, and look at this new addition which is destined to become a permanent fixture. Where did it come from, I wonder? How did it get here? Are the tomatoes too established to transplant? What color is it likely to be? Why is it here?

Within each life there are deep roots which can remain buried for a long time, then suddenly burst into our present. Some of these roots are biological, some behavioral, but almost all of them are older than we are. The Biblical assertion that the sins of the father are visited on the children has taken on new meaning in our age as we have learned more about families and the way they function. Like old azalea roots producing new growth in a garden, problems which families face in one generation frequently form the emotional agenda of later generations. We have long known about the intergenerational problems caused by alcoholism in a family, and we are increasingly aware of medical problems that find their foundation in genetic, not behavioral realities. The emotional and spiritual residue caused by incest and parental or spousal abuse lasts for generations.

What we know in theory, we often lose sight of in the garden of our own spirit. I work my own soul, digging, probing, trying to plant and encourage growth. Like the work in my garden, it is arduous, serious labor, often producing aches and pains. In the work, I become aware that many of the obstacles to my own development as a human being, a father, a husband, and a priest are seeds and roots long buried which spring to life unbidden, often at terribly inconvenient times, hindering or preventing the growth of something precious, deeply desired. My inability to pray as I should comes, I discover, from some ancient attempt to postulate the presence of a Sunday school God who is unable to deal with the anguish and worry of adult dilemmas. My lack of willingness to engage with a person or group comes, I find, not from the nature of their agenda or activity, but rather from long nursed fears of rejection and ridicule which I experienced as an adolescent. My rigidity with my children is grounded not in a lack of confidence in their maturity, but in my reaction to the parenting I received in a different age and time. My inability to follow through on projects I hunger to complete, my insensitivity to the needs of others, my reticence to yield to the expertise of those more skilled than myself—all these are rooted not in the excuses I provide for my own dislikes, but rather in some issue long buried in my own heart.

With each new act, I find I must deal with the actions of my own past.

Worse, I discover that I react not only out of my own history, but also out of generations of behavior which has preceded me in family, nation, and culture. Thus, while I would never count myself a racist, I find that I must be constantly engaged in overcoming the racism inherent in the society which gave me life, groomed me, and in which I function. I must engage *within myself* the bigotry, the lust for vengeance, the *de facto* godlessness which characterizes the world into which I was born.

Some of these I find so repugnant, so life threatening, that they require constant vigilance in keeping their seed and spawn out of my garden. With others, like the azalea, I have decided to allow some of the old growth to stand, not because it is where I want it to be, but because I am learning how to grow around it, how to accept the *givenness* of some of the contours of the human spirit. In a sense, I am learning to forgive myself for my own humanity, my own inability to make a perfect garden.

I have learned that some inclinations of the human heart are toxic enough to warrant single-minded dedication to their total elimination. I have also come to believe that there are others which must, to some degree, be tolerated in my spirit, ringed around, contained, but allowed to be, like a patch of mint which adds fragrance to the summer air, but which must be restricted to prevent its consuming everything around it. Appetite, the desire for pleasure, the enjoyment of others' praise and admiration, the temptation to extend rest to the level of sloth—like the azalea in my plum tomatoes, I am content to contain these while I focus my aggressive exorcism on those roots which threaten to undo my planting entirely.

But I have also found that with each passing year, and with continued effort, the ground requires less clearing than it did at first, and my prayer is that as I persevere, every aggressive growth may at last be removed.

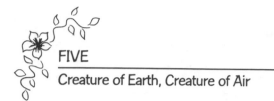

FIVE

Creature of Earth, Creature of Air

The lamppost in front of my parents' home supports a variegated blue and white clematis that is to die for. When it is in bloom in late spring and early summer, it can be seen a hundred yards away. Brilliant, riotous in its profusion and intensity, it looks like a fountain of color arising from the earth fully five feet in the air, then splaying into cascades of blossom and leaf. I enjoy it most in the evenings when the lamp is lit and the colors of the blossoms are backlit and radiant, a beacon of beauty on a dark and quiet street. With characteristic humility, my mother takes credit for nothing more than its planting, crediting its success to location alone. "I guess it just likes that spot," she says. In her economy of gardening, things flourish or fail primarily on the basis of their placement.

My clematis, on the other hand, have been pitiable things. One planted at the base of a stone column in front of the rectory a few years ago seemed to be headed in the right direction, but after a few weeks of promising growth, snaked into adjoining lilac bushes and refused to be redirected. Each week, I would retie new growth to the wire trellis around the column, but like a terrier routing out a fox's den, it willfully moved deeper into the lilacs. After a two-week vacation, I returned home to find that the vine had sensed my absence and wrapped itself so effectively around the lilac that there was nothing left but to cut it down and move the root ball to a new location. The clematis never came up again.

I have planted two in my backyard against our stockade fence. One promises a large white flower, the other a more compact burgundy blossom. In an act of hopefulness, I created a fan-shaped trellis of wire against the fence and waited for the vines to take off. As if mocking my optimism, the vines crept toward the base of the fan and sat for the rest of the summer, moving no further toward my dream of a wall of splendid color.

"Don't worry about them," my mother advised. "They'll come back next year as long as the root is alive. That is, as long as it's a good spot for them."

The things which grow in my garden are creatures of two worlds. Those two worlds couldn't be more dissimilar. One solid, tangible, malleable; the other insubstantial, immutable. They are creatures of earth and creatures of air. Even the most inexperienced gardener knows that it isn't enough to place seed in soil and hope for the best. The earth must be ready for the seed, and the seed must find hospitality and potential in the soil. Further, the sky to which the plant aspires must provide new growth with appropriate atmosphere. It must carry the life-giving rays of the sun, free of intrusive or limiting growth. Foul the soil or block the air and the plant dies. Find a place where soil is friable and rich, and the air unobstructed and you have what my mother calls "a good spot."

The plant itself makes use of both media, perfect in its capacity for symbiosis. Drawing nutrients from the soil, using the air around it for the miracle of photosynthesis, it is both a user and a contributor. Further, the soil and the air both benefit from its presence.

To be fair, lots of things grow in bad spots, but these are inevitably scraggly, the mutants in the plant world, managing to cling tenaciously to life but never reaching their potential. That they live at all is a testament to their versatility and adaptability.

I know souls like that—men and women who seem to have been deprived of something vital, essential for life. Like stunted plants struggling in bad spots, they display by their chronic irritability, their sourness, their cruelty, a life that has had to make do without some vital element. They sport malnourished spirits and, usually unwilling to confine their misery to the borders of their own spirits, tend to be contagious, freely spreading their pain around among the members of their family, the places where they work, or the groups they are involved with. I've seen plenty of them in life—folks who live to impose their will on others, people whose toxic behavior has the power to poison any group or undertaking.

I believe that like the plants in my garden, we too are creatures of earth, creatures of air: powerful amalgams of spirit and flesh that, just like garden growth, require sustenance from both sources. However, I have noticed that among the most emotionally stunted people, physical needs are rarely a problem—they have adequate resources to meet their needs for food, clothing, shelter, warmth. What they seem to lack is something decidedly spiritual, something nontangible which is essential for healthy human life. Respect, affection, support, encouragement—these are the necessities without which human life withers, distorts.

Some may claim that a lack of spiritual nutrition in childhood is the largest contributing factor. There is no doubt that all young growth needs proper nourishment to flourish. However, there is a greater truth which we must be bold enough to embrace and proclaim. Some lives refuse to accept the nourishment that is offered them. Some never make it to the font. Hold some sour spirit in your mind—perhaps a family member or a friend.

Is it possible that their misery could survive in the face of grace? Can any-one leave the presence of God, whether in prayer or worship, as unhappy as before they entered the divine presence without having missed some-thing essential?

Ultimately, we must accept responsibility for our own misery. If we find ourselves chronically dwarfed, stunted (assuming our pain is not gen-erated by the chemical processes of our own bodies) can it be because we have refused to drink deeply at the fountain of God's goodness? What shall we say of the troublemaker, the gossip, the liar? That they are to be tolerated or (worse) excused simply because they are in a bad spot? Must we not demand that they desist in the propagation of their own misery, inviting them to embrace fully the nourishment and strength to be had free for the asking from the bosom of God?

Such a demand for maturity is often lacking in the garden of contem-porary society. We yield to the behavioral terrorism of others, unwilling to confront the perpetrator of pain with the demand for maturity because it wouldn't be "nice" or "polite." In actual fact, "niceness" and "politeness" bother us very little. Our compliance with another's aggression is grounded in our own fear of these people, our own lack of confidence that we will be strong enough to assert our right to life without their pain and their respon-sibility to behave well. Of course, in the process, we ourselves become doubly poisoned—first by their aggression, and second, by our own feel-ings of inadequacy.

This becomes for us the greatest point of peril. In our tolerance of another's pain, we risk losing ourselves in the bargain—not our identity or our vocation or our family or home, but the essential part of our being which would flourish without restriction.

Jesus handled these folks so well. He didn't need techniques or word formulas invented by pop psychology, nor did he depend on manipulation. He did two things. First, he refused to embrace their anger or cruelty and incorporate it into himself. Second, he spoke truthfully with them—no plati-tudes, no cajoling or bargaining, just the simple truth about their behavior and his goodness. "Why are you condemning her when you yourselves have sinned?" "It's your hardness of heart that made this commandment necessary." How shocking, how bold the truth sounds in the face of enmity, yet how that truth has the power to clear the air! Unlike us, Jesus always demanded that people accept responsibility for their own behavior, de-manding also that they be prepared for the consequences of that behavior.

I stand before the wilting clematis that I have planted and hold my mother's vine in mind. To be sure, I planted badly. I look around for a "good spot" where it might flourish next year and in so doing, pledge to explore the good spots I create within my own spirit.

SIX

The Suprise That Comes When Confidence Mounts

I am on a roll. On my hands and knees, sweat dripping from my brow, I move along the edge of my peppermint pink impatiens, pulling weeds at warp speed. The soil is loose, slightly moist, and the roots of these intruders come out easily. The air around me is cool, the sun is shining overhead, and I'm doing a bang-up job. I look at the border stretched before me with beds yet to be cleared and a sense of confidence builds in me that this portion of the garden will be restored to pristine beauty in less than an hour. Already, I am living out my next fantasy—reclining in my lawn chaise under the shade of my dogwood (a little wren furiously bringing sticks to the bird bottle which hangs from the tree's branches), baseball game on the radio, fully relaxed in the midst of my garden enjoying the dividends of my labor.

My mood is expansive, ebullient. How could there be anything more productive, more satisfying than working in concert with the earth, enjoying its benevolence? Here we are, nature and I, working in harmony—she opening herself to me, me grooming her, devoted to her continuing beauty. My hands work, my mind sings.

Pain! Searing pain! My left hand, across my palm, each finger, burning, pointed, sharp, silver pain, running to my armpit. I've grabbed something. Something sharp, sharp in many places, running down the length of my hand. First I look at earth, that vixen come to seduce me into ruin and see a noxious spike of stem with a thousand thorns along its length. No leaf in sight, just needlelike deep piercing shards of misery and disfigurement.

I look at my hand. Never one to wear gloves, I curse my own inattentiveness to the work before me. Now there are thirty or forty needle shafts along my palm extending to each swelling length of finger. Foolishly, I try to pull them out quickly, only to have the protruding shaft snap off at the skin, leaving dozens of silken slivers embedded in my hand. Whatever nettle this might be, it loves revenge and now I watch as my sore hand begins to redden and swell with rage at this intruder's toxic sting.

21

The weeding stops, and while I repair to the chaise under the dogwood, it isn't with a glass of ice tea and a sense of thrill at the gentle breeze, but with tweezers, ointment, needle and magnifier. This isn't the worst that life has to offer, but it's bad enough: my hand throbs throughout this exorcism, and beside me the Phillies are losing to the Mets on the radio.

There is no more dangerous time for a Christian than the time of contentment. We frequently feel that the most perilous moments are ones when we are caught in the midst of a great upheaval, when the events of life swirl around us leaving us numbed with confusion or pain. Death, illness, a crisis in the life of a child—we fear that these are the times when we are most vulnerable, most likely to lose our connection to God. But I have found that the evil one is remarkably ineffective during such times—times when, in our distress, we long to draw nearer to the heart of God and throw ourselves into the Spirit's care. But when things go well, when we are convinced of the invulnerability of life's goodness—these are the moments the devil loves.

A real devil, with a personality? The rational, intellectual part of me cries NO, of course not. My wounded hand screams yes. I am a poor theologian and a worse metaphysician, but I have come to embrace the truth of Saint Paul's assertion that we contend against principalities and powers which we cannot begin to visualize. I have, on more than one occasion, been convinced that I was caught in a vortex of genuine evil, of a malevolent presence in which my security and well-being was threatened, endangered. Because of my emotional makeup, indeed my very humanity, I have seen those moments as being intensely personal, as though this force beyond my describing had hunted me down, took aim at my soul and fired its most deadly weapon. It has seemed to me to be a predator, I have felt myself its prey.

But I have noticed that this power has been most aggressive when I myself have begun to depend on my own resource rather than the goal of understanding myself as a child of God. I suppose that the difference between the two is not clear for many people in this age of The Individual. The culture that promotes the phrases "If it feels good, do it," or "My body is my own to do with as I please" finds it difficult to understand the individual as anything more than a single unit, free of obligation to others, free of interdependency. Yet I believe that the Gospel provides a radically different definition of human life. The message of Jesus is that we are not, in fact, self-contained islands, free of the demands of mutuality. Rather, we are people in *relationship*: first, with our God, then with those whose lives touch our own. As unpopular as it will sound in a time of self-determination and self-actualization, we exist in an atmosphere of connectedness, where every act, every thought somehow affects not only those around us, but our creator as well.

Some will object that this understanding of human life as adjectival to divine life is unhealthy, akin to emotional and behavioral slavery. In actuality, it is tremendously liberating. I no longer am forced to deal with the demands of life with the few resources I have within my personal "toolbox." The assertion of television talk shows and self-help books that the ability to live life well depends solely on our acquisition of more behavioral skills belies the paucity of this approach. If the truth were told, we are unable to acquire enough information or personal skill to meet all of life's crises. It is when I try to act as the pop psychers insist, depending on me and my acquired knowledge only, that the evil one makes the deepest inroads into my spirit.

Thanks be to God, I am free from being condemned to the arrogance of individuality! But, wait! That freedom also means that I am a man under obligation. I am, as the great Jewish theologian Martin Buber once said, "willed for the life of communion." It is only within that communion that I find the resource to face the worst life has to offer, only in that communion that I have at my disposal the power and ability of the Holy One. But even more, my relationship as a dependent child of God does more than give me access to information or skill, as though God were little more than a computer's on-line encyclopedia. Rather, it becomes the model for other relationships in which I am engaged. Because I am the recipient of all God has to offer, I have not only the ability, but the obligation to be self-offering, self-emptying, self-available as a husband, a father, a friend, a priest. I even have the ability to act that way as a stranger met by others—wasn't that the point of the parable of the good Samaritan?

I wish I could say that this was a relationship which, once entered, was permanent and unshakable. But I too often embrace willfulness and self-reliance like a weeder who abandons caution. I spend much of my life somewhere in between these two poles, caught in the tension of someone longing to be God's, yet someone cursed by a base hunger to act alone. Until I yield completely, I am condemned to spend time nursing the thorns in my spirit.

SEVEN

My Companions in the Garden

I love the birds. I'm not a dedicated birder who travels to a neighboring state to tramp through the salt marsh in hopes of seeing something rare to add to my "life list." Instead, I love to sit in my garden and look at my avian neighbors as they sail from branch to branch. There are no exotic birds in my garden, at least none that I have seen. Like most other people in our area, we have the standard assortment of chickadees, titmice, sparrows, jays, and robins. The winter brings purple thrush to the feeder along with the cardinals who aren't as apparent in the summer months, but whose characteristic *chee-chee* can be heard just about everywhere. Occasionally I'll see something remarkable if not rare—a Baltimore oriole or a streak of airborne yellow as a goldfinch streaks by. There's a great horned owl in the neighborhood which the crows help me spot once or twice a year. On one remarkable morning a few years ago, an owlet sat in a dogwood branch above my garden for the better part of half an hour until it couldn't take the attention which my wife and I showered on her any more and flew off to a more private perch.

The wrens seem most sociable. Each year we hang out a hollow gourd or two, and they come willingly, spending untold hours like tireless construction workers, using twigs and the yarn and hair we leave out to make our humble gourds a fit home for their young. They don't seem to mind the activity in the garden in the summer months, and will watch with what I am convinced is rapt fascination as I weed and prune, cut and trim. I, in turn, watch their display of courage when the jays come to raid their nests. Here, some plump but tiny little wren defends her home against the blue jay's intrusion despite the jay's superior size, reach, and strength. Like a good soldier establishing a safe perimeter for an encampment, the wren has drawn an imaginary circle around her home, and should one of our cats violate that circle in an attempt to stretch out on the lawn in the summer sun, the wren swoops down from the tree, diving to within a foot or two of the cat, making her ownership of the airspace above the area clear.

There has never been a circus star more entertaining than the Downey woodpeckers who skitter up and down the trees in my garden, nor a cowboy more bold and daring than the flicker (complete with a red bandana!), who enters the garden each time as if it were a wilderness waiting to be tamed.

I try not to romanticize or sentimentalize the birds—I don't speak of them as Beatrix Potter characters or imagine them as anything more than the other creatures in my garden like the mouse or mole or spider. They are, like my less mobile neighbors, simply doing what we all do—making home, mating, seeking shelter from the storm, raising their young, looking for enough to eat. But unlike the squirrel or the tick, the birds delight the eye, inspire longing, prick my imagination. They are, to me, like flying candy, color on the wing that flashes across the ubiquitous green of leaf and lawn. My garden—still, ordinary, stationary—is suddenly invaded by a flash of brilliant yellow or searing red. I can't remember a moment when I wasn't surprised by the arrival of a bird, even though the surprise was momentary, followed by the acceptance born of recognition. "There! What's that? Oh yes, the jay. He'll be after the wren's eggs, no doubt." I've never seen a bird in the corner of my eye and failed to look, even if only for an instant. It's something spontaneous, automatic, I suppose. Movement, quick identification, return to task.

The birds also have a special place in my memory—a kind of "right to residence." I see them only for the briefest of times—one second, three, five? Yet I remember their crossing my line of sight far more readily than the passing of an automobile when I am on the road, or the verbal list of sundries my wife asks me to pick up from the store. Hours, days after such a sighting I will say to my family or a friend, "Oh, I saw the oriole the other day. Such a brilliant orange set in all the green of the sycamore!" They then smile, thinking (and remembering!) the orioles they have seen and loved in the seeing.

In many ways, the movement of the birds through my life is similar to the appearance of God. I can't speak for others, but God most often becomes present to me in the same fleeting way that the birds fly through my garden. I have had very few moments where I have sensed and enjoyed God's abiding. I do not intend to imply that God is not constantly present to us, but rather that my awareness of God's presence is momentary, rather than enduring. At the Eucharist, in prayer with a friend, while nursing my memory or confronting a problem or pain, "Ah! Of course! God is here. This is a holy moment." Like the flight of a goldfinch across my line of sight, these experiences are never taken for granted, but are always surprising, startling. Just as the swath of green leaf is shattered by the sudden red flare of a cardinal's movement, God always breaks through the ordinariness of the moment, forcing me to stop, look, pay attention. In the same way that the sight of one Downey sparks the memory of other woodpeckers, the arrival of the divine moment always connects me to my own holy history—those places and times when God shattered the unremitting sameness of my own inattentiveness and demanded that I look more carefully at what was happening around me.

Like the gliding path of the sparrow hawk or the acrobatics of a chickadee, these divine invasions into my self-absorption rarely last long. Rather, they are God's "in and out" reminders to me not to stray far from the awareness of the holiness which saturates the world around me.

Like my "backyard birding," there has been nothing terribly exotic or rare about God's visitation of me in my spirit-space. There have been a few remarkable moments, like the arrival of the great horned owl, but nothing dramatic or extraordinary. I have no doubt but that these moments exist in the lives of others, just as I know that there are those who will climb high mountains at the risk of great personal danger to catch a fleeting glimpse of some wonderful winged creature which few humans have ever seen. Instead, my experience in the garden of God has been much the same as many of those around me, or at least it has been what others might experience if they spent more time in the garden of the human spirit as they do in other places. If my sightings have not been spectacular, they have certainly been frequent, consistent, and deeply satisfying. And they have provided me with the extraordinary joy of knowing that the God who covers the earth and fills the air with glory comes near to me often, and longs to be seen.

EIGHT

In Season and Out of Season

It's late in the day on a gray November afternoon. I have just walked through my garden in the same way an old man walks through his memories. There's very little that remains of summer's growth—five scrawny leeks left behind like uncoordinated kids, condemned to watch a sandlot baseball game they weren't chosen to play in, wilting impatiens, a handful of baby string beans which if not picked would be killed by the hard frost predicted for tonight. Hands thrust deep in my pockets, I look at my empty beds. No weeds cry out to be pulled. No vines bend over needing to be tied to stakes. No flowers to be picked for the table, no broad leaves hiding the surprise of an unseen squash.

The temptation to walk away is strong, heading for the warmth of the house and the embrace of pastimes more suited to winter days and nights. The feeling arises from my personality, being the kind of person who likes to push for closure then move onto the next project. I am, I think, a problem solver by nature rather than a maintenance man. I like to have things done, completed, moving quickly to embrace that most exciting of realities, The Next Thing. And so I shrug, as much from the biting wind as from resignation, and call the dog back to the door and to his supper.

Even as I move into the warmth of the house, I know that my work in the garden has not ended simply because there is nothing left to harvest. There is as much work to be done now that the growing season has ended as there ever was during the height of the summer months. While the temptation is strong to turn my back on the earth and wait for spring when I can again focus on produce and flower, there is another reality to consider.

This garden has spent itself at my direction for six months. The requirements I have placed upon it have leeched the nourishment from the soil, altered the chemical composition of the earth itself. I have taken freely from it, now I must return what I have taken. The work that extends before me carries little of the pleasure I derive from gardening in fruitful months. Rather, this is the time of hard labor and no product. There are leaves to be raked, shredded, and turned into the soil. The lifeless tomato vines, pepper plants, wilted zucchini leaves and broccoli stems need to be chopped and composted. The hollows and mounds of the planting places have to be evened out. Dead branches in the surrounding trees need to be cut out, chipped, and folded into the planting beds. I will comb the soil for unharvested potatoes which will provide me with eyes for next year's planting. The vining roses and butterfly bush will be cut back to encourage new and stronger growth next year.

The work is unpleasant. My hands will become raw with the cold; the wind will find ways through my coat and leave me chilled. The dank wetness of the soil will surround my feet despite the heavy soles of my shoes and the insulated socks I wear. The soil should be turned before its winter sleep so that the rain and snow can find their way beneath its surface without pooling in the compacted paths I walked between the planting.

And then there's the planning. I chart out this summer's growth so that I know where to place new young things next year. All the crops will be rotated to different areas next spring to evenly distribute the requirements placed on the soil.

Some plants will be dug up, potted and pruned in an attempt to nurse them through the winter months—a favorite gardenia, some geraniums, the hibiscus. I'll bring the impatiens in, knowing that they probably will not make it to spring, but in the hopes that I can enjoy their color for a while longer.

Hard stuff, this autumn gardening, and work I don't really enjoy. It's the work of cut and patch and mend, and carries few of the rewards of summer's effort. But unpleasant and arduous as it is, it is part of the work, and I honor it. It is part of the covenant I have with the garden, to see to its needs so that it can see to mine. The doing of the work marks the difference between a gardener and an opportunist.

In that sense, my covenant with the garden is not unlike my covenants, my solemn promises, with other people in my life. I had, over the course of my life, made a number of vows, of solemn promises. I have vowed, through the sacrament of confirmation, to uphold promises made in my name as an infant to embrace Christianity alone out of all the powerful forces at work in the world. I have vowed to be a husband to my wife through the sacrament of holy matrimony. I have vowed to be a Christian guardian of another's life through the sacrament of holy baptism. I have vowed to embrace both a diaconal and a priestly ministry through the sacrament of ordination. I have made other vows of a purely secular nature, like the promise to fulfill a financial obligation. All of these vows entail work, all promise personal reward.

Ours seems to be a society which no longer values the solemnity of promises. In fact, I believe we have come to that unfortunate state where we spend more effort providing accessible routes for the dissolution of promises than we do in preparing ourselves for the act of engaging in solemn vows. In this rush to dispensation, we also have shed any feeling of personal responsibility for our failure to fulfill our covenants. Marriages are readily and inexpensively dissolved through a process which bears the oxymoronic name "no-fault divorce." Unwanted pregnancies are terminated under the aegis of insurance carriers who list the procedure in the euphemistic category of "health maintenance." Bankruptcy is advertised as the solution to a variety of financial problems. Crime carries consequence only if the criminal's representation fails in finding the appropriate legal loophole.

I believe that the church itself has failed in demanding accountability of those who enter into the solemnity of sacramental covenants. We baptize as a social convention, irrespective of the parents' or godparents' commitment to faithful living as Christian men and women. We rush to fill our confirmation classes with children who have not been inside the church since their own baptism, and are not likely to return until their wedding. We consent to marry men and women who seek out a church simply because they like its appearance or its proximity to their reception hall. Our willingness to perform such "sacraments without substance" is a result of the church's tragic need to feel successful, close to the glory days of the 1950s when pews were full and Sunday schools burst at the seams. Since that time, the church has appeared to be in decline, like a garden in autumn where no fruit is produced. Clergy blame congregations for their lack of enthusiasm or the failure of their efforts in personal evangelism. People blame their clergy because of lackluster preaching or the failure of parish programs to attract outsiders. Observers and commentators point to changes in liturgy or the evolving practices of denominations in ordaining people who have traditionally been at the margins of society. The fingers of blame point this way and that, but the decline continues.

Can it be that the church is in decline because Christians have turned their back on the hard work of cultivating their spirits? Our times are characterized by spectacles, extravaganzas in the media, in the public square and in our entertainment. We have become a people accustomed to quick and satisfying results in everything from food preparation to pain relievers. The winter work of spiritual development is decidedly slow, tedious and hard. Consequently, many people put aside the foundational work of careful preparation and attentive cultivation. Quick spiritual fixes look attractive and promising, so people turn this way and that as each new spiritual fad emerges from wishing on crystals to the mumbling of mantras. Each of these spiritual fads has the power to captivate public interest in time, but then they inevitably disappear as people realize that like most quick solutions to deep problems, they have no staying power.

Work at prayer, attentive study of the Word of God, constancy in worship, faithfulness in stewardship, dedication to kindness and compassion— this is the stuff of which fruitful souls are made. But it is hard, frustrating work, decidedly unsatisfying for those who want their spirituality, like their meals, ready in an instant. By our very nature we are impatient, lazy, prone to accepting less as long as it can be produced quickly. But if we want fast results in our personal lives, we want it in our institutional life as well.

Truth be told, the people of God, both lay and ordained, have let the church lie fallow, like a garden ignored after the harvest has been reaped. Because the work of preparation and tending seems hard and fruitless, we have abandoned the arduous work required out of season. Instead, we jump from program to program, investing our faith in quick fixes like some kind of ecclesiastical patent elixir.

This is no cry for a return to old time religion. The times in which we live require bold, creative new ways of proclaiming the Good News of God in Jesus Christ, but those bold new methods of proclamation require that the work of tending, preparation, and investment of the people of God be done faithfully and well.

Where do we begin? Like careful gardeners who prepare to tend fallow ground, I believe that we must begin with faithful clergy who love their people. While there is much to be said for effective programs and efficient administration, the church must never hope to revive itself on the basis of its success as an organization. We are first and foremost a community, a family, and families thrive on love, not method. There is deep wisdom in the assertion of Saint Paul that a little leaven leavens the whole lump, and the church of God in Jesus Christ has rarely seemed as lump-like as it is now. Inert, inactive, uncertain of its own boundaries, this lump is in desperate need of good leaven, and that leaven is love. Clergy have within their capacity and their sphere of responsibility the power to unleash unlimited love for the people they serve. But if they abrogate that opportunity in favor of the implementation of self-actualization workshops or administrative minutia, they condemn their congregations to the same organizational breakdown which has characterized the other lackluster and dysfunctional institutions in our society.

It is love we need, and love we lack. Not just affection or earnest feeling, but the kind of self-giving servant love which characterized the life of the one we call Lord. Funny thing about love—it can't be programmed or developed or implemented. It can only be given by one person to one person, and it is always costly. It costs the giver, and it costs the one who receives it. As long as our clergy spend more time in conferences and meetings than they do with their people, their churches must be condemned to organizationalism. I know that this assertion sounds naive and simplistic in the face of the church's current investment in sophisticated methods of group management and peer process. But I believe it is precisely these commitments which have failed us in our desperate hunger to regain a measure of organizational success which we believe we have lost. It has been my experience that when one ordained person is dedicated to loving and serving the needs of the individuals in his or her congregation, that congregation receives a kind of power to extend that care toward each other and those in need outside the limits of their family. If it seems naive to think that the clergy can affect such a change, it is a naivete born of ancient Anglican wisdom. When constructing the 1549 Book of Common Prayer, Archbishop Thomas Cranmer placed the burden of personal godliness squarely on the shoulders of clergy, insisting that they be conversant with scripture and so "be stirred up to godliness themselfes, and be more able also to exhorte others by wholsome doctrine, and to confute them that are adversaries to the trueth."

But the work of winter gardening is not restricted to the ordained. Just as the clergy have an obligation to the congregation, so the laity have a greater obligation to the church throughout the world—after all, the church's ministry belongs to all the baptized, not just the ordained. If the church flounders at the hands of inept or misdirected leaders, it is primarily because the laity have abrogated their ownership of the Body of Christ and applied to the church standards of evaluation which they have imported from the worlds of finance, business, and politics. If the starting point of our revitalization is the love of clergy for their congregations, its genesis will be when people demand to be loved. If the church languishes because of tired preaching or a bankrupt stewardship, Christians must rise and demand inspiration of their leaders. In the parable of the importunate widow, a woman who has been denied justice because she is on the outer boundaries of the legal system persistently berates a judge until he grants her justice. Certainly, this parable has a more universal application than the plight of the bereaved in our civil courts. If the leadership of a congregation has lapsed into mundanity, the people of God betray their faith if they simply turn their back on the garden and walk away leaving, as Archbishop Runcie once said, "the bland to lead the bland." The failure of leadership is not only attributable to the inadequacy of the leader, but to the complacency of those who are led.

To be sure, much more than this is needed, but I believe it is the best place to start. This radical revision of the church's agenda will be difficult at first. Like the gardener faced with the tasks attending a fruitless garden, the establishment of the law of love in a congregation where only a commitment to activity has existed may seem daunting, intimidating. But only a little leaven is needed before the lump responds.

NINE

There's a Hammock in My Garden Where I Think About My Death

There is a point along Interstate 95 just south of Dillon, South Carolina where the billboards advertising the South of the Border Motel stop ("Pedro sez...") and the billboards advertising Pawley's Island hammocks begin. A Pawley's Island hammock is a wonderful thing. Woven of cotton rope, it supports the body evenly while letting the warm summer breeze surround the lucky user both top and bottom. It sags and stretches to meet the body's contours, but after every rain, shrinks back to its original state so that a family is never condemned to the consequences of one person's use.

I have a Pawley's Island hammock in my backyard, stretched on a tubular steel frame which allows me to move it around the garden in search of the longest stretch of sun. At one end I have tied a large red canvas bolster pillow. For fully three seasons of the year I am always aware of the presence of the hammock in my garden, no matter where I am or what I am doing. More than a comfortable remembrance, the hammock is a constant siren that calls to me alluringly, inviting me to rest. When I succumb, it yields to my body, rocks me gently, demands that I set aside the care of daily life.

My hammock feels best after a prolonged period of work, whether that work is in the garden or the office. Part of that feeling is the covenant I have made with myself to make "hammock time" free of the obligations of my day. I have trained myself to clear my mind of every urgency, promising myself that these pressing things will be waiting for me after I stand up. As a result, the time I spend there is like a little retreat, a welcome interlude in the course of what is too often a hectic day.

But as anyone who has ever been on one will attest, a productive retreat is not an escape. Rather, it is a time to withdraw for a while, re-group, reexamine issues and priorities, and set an agenda for the coming days. Some go on retreats to enrich their prayer lives, others to cultivate their spiritual selves, still others to deepen their sensitivity to the pain of others. When I am in my hammock, I think about my death.

Death is a constant companion for the gardener. Not only do we watch our plantings die when the killing frost arrives, we ourselves uproot them as soon as they no longer bear fruit in order to make room for newer, more promising seedlings. We chop them into bits and throw them on the compost heap and wait for decay to leave us with rich humus. We take down trees that have had a long life to create light for shaded plants or space for new beds. We destroy living things—flying things, crawling things, creeping things, which threaten the life of other things which we have planted. The gardener kills to produce, the gardener kills to protect, the gardener kills to preserve, but throughout the year, the gardener kills.

But this isn't real death, is it? Watching a plant die or engineering the death of bugs certainly can't be compared to real death, the death of people, can it?

I spend a fair amount of time with the dying. One of the things I do for a living is the planning and celebration of funerals. Whenever death comes, whoever death touches, death leaves an emotional bruise. Sometimes that bruise is deep, terribly damaging, almost life threatening, just as when a person is in an automobile accident and their heart or liver is bruised. Very often, these bruises leave scars which last as long as an individual lives, often affecting the way they function. At other times, the extent of the bruise is not as great, and the healing that is necessary to return the body to full health is not long coming. But I have never witnessed a death that did not hurt someone, somewhere. Really hurt.

Many of the people I visit know that they are near to death. Either they have been told or they have a deep inner sense that does not require telling. Most of them are afraid. Some of them weep incessantly from a deep sadness. A few are resigned. There are others who feel nothing, simply because we medicate our dying to the extent that they are free of the impact of emotion. I've never been entirely certain about whether we do this for the dying or for ourselves.

When I visit people who are close to their own death, many want to talk. At times, they express regret about opportunities missed, or things they wish they hadn't done. They often express their concern for those who will live after them, worrying about the loneliness of a spouse or a caretaker child. Sometimes they want to rehearse earthly moments of pleasure or joy, walking through bittersweet memories, pointing out pleasant places along the way. Some have asked questions about God or about heaven, or about their own ultimate disposition.

The dying often slip in and out of consciousness, and many talk to me about the sense they have about what's coming next. For some, it is as though they slide back and forth between two worlds just before their dying, seeing what's ahead, returning to that which is behind. They speak of light, and of seeing others who have died before them, and the beauty of the One who is just ahead of them.

None of these conversations are pleasant. If we were enjoying tea and scones on a broad swath of lawn sitting in fancy wrought iron patio furniture, I might enjoy it more. But when I talk to these folks, they are in a hospital bed with machines whirring around them, and they often struggle to speak around tubes or a tongue that's too dry. Their mouths and eyes and noses are crusted. Their bodies reek of the death which is spreading through their organs in the same way that green fog moved through the streets of Egypt in *The Ten Commandments*. Their hair is matted, their hands and feet unwashed. Their skin is slack and cold to the touch. For every coherent sentence there may be ten that aren't, or mumbling which I cannot understand. When I look at their faces, their bodies, there is little or no resemblance to the person I knew months or weeks or, at times, even days before.

Usually, we're in the room alone. The medical staff has all the information they need on a monitor at the nurses' station. The family is often in and out, unable to bear this scene for long stretches. Cleaning folks come in, sweep around the bed and leave. I tend to stay, an hour, sometimes two. I anoint them with holy oil, as if to give them a final grooming for their arrival. I hold a hand or stroke a brow or touch a cheek, just so our skin meets. I say the prayers for the dying, I often hum or sing softly, knowing that hearing is often the last sense to leave. Old hymns, mostly—hymns they would have known, even if they haven't done any hymn singing since Sunday school days. Abide with me, fast falls the even tide, the darkness deepens, Lord with me abide. O Lord, my God, when I in awesome wonder consider all the worlds thy hands have made. O God, our help in ages passed, our hope for years to come, our shelter from the stormy blast, and our eternal home. When we've been there ten thousand years, bright, shining as the sun; we've no less days to sing God's praise than when we'd first begun.

There are times when I am fortunate and they leave before I have to. Other times, more painful times, I have to say goodbye.

I bring these moments to my hammock in temperate months, rehearse them, go over them like an old Mohammedan jiggling worry beads. And I put myself in that bed with crusty eyes and labored breath and folks rushing past my door on errands for those who can yet be saved. And I judge whether I am living well. Well enough to be at peace, alone, when the breathing stops and the heart's at rest and the hymns are sung by clearer voices than my own.

All this takes place in my garden, that space where death comes each year, where I watch the soil emerge from the cold shroud of winter white and spring to new life in an endless series of miracles. I expect that in the eternal economy, God is the ultimate gardener, making new life out of old dead things day after day. And at the time when my old body of death will be turned back into the soil, I will not be surprised when I inherit a new life which cannot die.

TEN

The Gardener Isn't God

The morning was perfect. Sitting on the patio with first coffee in my hand and the paper in my lap, I scanned the sky above me only to find it spotless—not a cloud in sight. The cool air of the late spring meant that I would be able to work throughout the morning without feeling tired. I might even get a little sun. Warming my hands on the outside of the cup, I planned the morning's work. There were some perennials to put in—a Stella D'Oro lily, a black-eyed Susan, three delphiniums and a daisy, all of which were culled by a friend from her garden. Flats of herbs bought the previous day needed to be set out. I had some small stumps to dig out from an area I had just cleared, and I was planning to cut a section of the arbor vitae back to the ground to promote even growth. Sunflower seeds to plant. Aim the weed whacker between the bricks on the path. A long hot shower.

I suppose that those who have no taste for yard work wouldn't believe the deep sense of pleasure that came with the effort. To some it might seem like drudgery born of obligation. In fact, I'm certain that there are days when it might seem so to me. But on that day, in that spring, in that yard, the work was sheer delight. The soil opened for my planting, freely gave up the long roots and stumps of shrubs I had removed weeks before. Cutting down the arbor vitae (always a joy in itself) seemed effortless. I worked to the accompaniment of the wren's whistle, stopped from time to time to take long swigs of water, watched my refuse pile grow with satisfaction. There was enough sweat on my brow to feel good, enough of a breeze to refresh me.

It starts as a mild sensation of hunger. "Must be close to lunchtime," I say aloud. But unlike my body's usual call for food, the sensation moves up into my rib cage instead of lower in my abdomen. Who knows? Gas, fatigue, thirst, too much sun. Now it is in my head and my arms, and I know there is something wrong. It moves more quickly than I can and I am overwhelmed by a feeling of panic, of lightheadedness, of detachment from my surroundings as though my brain was pulling back from my body into a deeper recess, hiding from life. I am already on my way to the house, having let shovel and rake drop to the ground. Before I can make the door, I am completely overcome by the panic, the urgent screaming of my body, "Something's wrong! Something's wrong!" In thirty seconds, I have been reduced to powerlessness. I begin to fear that I will not have the strength to pull the door open and the dog, thinking I must be heading inside for the sole purpose of getting him something to eat, tangles himself around my legs. My knees, already weak, wobbly, twist around his bulky frame and I am on the ground, breathing hard, trying to raise myself on all fours. Pulling the storm door outward, I crawl through the doorway into the kitchen pantry. I open the nearest cupboard and reach for the box closest to hand— cereal. I tried to negotiate the top but my hands were weak, trembling too much to pry loose the flaps, so I tore at the box until I produced a hole in the side and I ate. Frantically.

There are many reasons why I garden. I enjoy the fresh air, I like the feeling of working the land, but most of all, I garden to produce. I produce flowers for my home or to beautify the land, and I produce vegetables for my family's table. This last reason is paramount. I garden to provide food for my family. It can be argued (with some success) that the vegetables I produce are more expensive than those which I could buy, especially considering the time invested. This is no doubt true. If I *really* wanted cucumbers or radishes or green beans, I could have them without waiting and for a modest cost at the local greengrocer. However, my vegetables are the work of my hands, produced by the sweat of my brow, nurtured and defended and coddled during my time. When we eat my produce, it tastes sweeter not because it is fresh from the garden, but because it is a direct result of my work.

In addition, the vegetables that I grow connect me to the intention of nature. While I am not a vegetarian, I do have a strong sense that there is a wisdom in creation. This wisdom allows the earth to provide for all the dietary needs of human life without the destruction of animals or birds or fish. When I eat from the earth, I provide for my body without destroying the body of another animate thing. I cannot avoid the truths provided by contemporary scientific insight that when I move outside the realm of that which is grown for food, I endanger my health. All the dietary evils known to humans seem to derive from one of two sources—the consumption of non-plant-based foods or the alteration of foods into derivative products. The message of nutritionists seems to be very clear—eliminate animal fats and processed foods and add significantly to your life and health.

I am not arguing for a society of vegetarians. I am well aware that we depend on the ability of livestock to convert the vegetation available to them from nonarable land into readily available protein. But at the same time, I have a deep knowing that this is the way it is supposed to be— people living from the bounty of the land, sharing the earth with animals who provide assistance with labor, milk, fertilizer and companionship.

Unfortunately, I don't live that way. Like most other people, my table sports as many spareribs and roast chicken and hamburgers as it does eggplant sesame casserole or green beans and rice. In fact, my tastes run as much to fast food as it does to slow food—the food which I plant and tend and harvest. But my body doesn't handle the meat-based, fat-laden, sugar-stuffed meals I enjoy as well as it does the leafy greens and beta-carotene rich vegetables which I delight in producing.

That fact, and a genetic predisposition, has resulted in diabetes. Among other things, my diabetes means that my sugar levels vary from day to day if I do not maintain tight control of my intake of fatty, sugar-laden foods. It means that episodes of hypoglycemia, like the one I experienced in my garden, come far too often if I neglect the business of serious self-care. God may be able to make things grow 24 hours a day, but I must stop, provide for my body's needs, care for my weakness in order to remain strong.

Consequently, my garden has taken on a new meaning for me. It is no longer just a source of food or a place to work. It is a symbol of my salvation as well. My investment in the garden, in the exercise it provides and the food It produces, becomes the source of my health, and my commitment to a stronger, healthier body.

But I am like Saint Paul. In his letter to Christians in the fledgling church in Rome, Paul examines the paradox which exists within himself. "For I do not do what I want, but I do the very thing I hate." The very thing which I need for health and wholeness I abandon in favor of that which has the power to do me harm. Caught between taste and desire, I swing like a weight on a string between my sinful desires and my longing for health. This makes me appear to be at war with myself, caught in an unending conflict between longing and desire.

Most people live with that kind of conflict every day. The most broken among us are those who are unable to forgive their swings between life and self-destruction. On the surface, this behavior seems illogical at best, indicative of moral or behavioral weakness at worst. For many centuries, human predilection for self-destructive behaviors has been condemned, scorned. It is only in the latter half of the twentieth century that we have discovered that such behaviors are largely not a result of moral or spiritual weakness, but rather are more deeply imbedded in our fundamental humanity. Our addictions, our appetites, our infirmities, our longings—many of these arise not from the mind or spirit of humans, but from their very flesh—from the cellular blueprints we carry within each living cell in our bodies. We are born with this desire for death and like long buried things which rise to the surface of the earth, our appetite for our own death rises from our body depths to dominate our mental and behavioral agenda. Deep within ourselves, we rage at this sentence of the generations handed down to do us. We fight against the injustice of having to do battle with the pains of our forebears or else we yield to do the inevitability of our own demise. "What can I do?" we ask. "I was born this way." But even those who have accepted the inevitability of the sentence long for deliverance. Saint Paul considers his own sinfulness: "O wretched man that I am," he cries, allowing us to do see the depth of his anguish. "Who shall deliver me from the body of this death?"

His pain should not blind us to the certainty of his hope. There *is* deliverance to be had, freedom from our own genetic past to be gained. "I thank God through Jesus Christ our Lord," he sighs, and we can almost hear the release of grateful breath across the ages. Somehow in God, we find the means of dealing with the conflict that rages within us. God alone is not the solution, anymore than God is the solution to sin or hatred or warfare. Rather, God is the vehicle through which we find the resolution of our distress. Here at last is help, here at last is promise.

But then Saint Paul says something which sounds strange to do modern ears. "So with my mind I serve the law of God," he says, "but with my body I serve the law of sin." Paul isn't implying that we are people divided, with one-half of our being acting one way and the other half acting a different way. For Saint Paul, the mind was more than a mechanism for thinking, it was the very essence of the self, the part of our being which sets the course for our life. The body must follow the course which is set by the conscious part of our selves, in much the same way that the caboose follows where the engine leads. Saint Paul is saying that while his body may be unruly (like a mule that wants to go its own way), the single-minded dedication of the whole self to do the law of God holds out the promise that such unruly wills can be tamed, transformed by the Spirit of God present and active in human life.

Herein lies the paradox of the Christian life. In order to conquer, we must first surrender. In order to win, we first must lose. "Dying to self," Jesus calls this process. We must embrace not only the method, but also the agenda of another, incorporate it into self, discarding our agenda along the way. I think this is what Christians mean when they say that one must accept Jesus Christ as Savior, as Lord. We do not mean slavish acceptance of some philosophy imposed on our lives, but rather, that we have come to realize that left to our own devices, our fleshly agenda is likely to win out and we will be destroyed. We have found a health, a vitality, a way of living in Jesus of Nazareth so obviously superior to do the forces of self-destruction which rules our own bodies that in order to live, we must yield.

As I must yield. I must yield to do the natural wisdom of which my garden is an icon and allow the old me which imposes itself on my spirit from countless generations of deathly practice to die.

ELEVEN

Christianity and the Wonderful Weed

I am deep in December. Outside the window above my desk the steady snow which began in the dark hours of morning is beginning to subside. There is a fire in the woodstove and the children have just finished decorating the Christmas tree. Our tree this year is lopsided—a crooked trunk leaving the top of the tree pointing toward Pittsburgh. I like it.

The house is filled with decorations, each one a symbol of the season or the faith which founded it. Wreaths, stars, trees, angels, shepherds and sheep, Magi and gifts. It is a season of powerful symbols, each meant to spark some thought of devotion or adoration, leading me to believe that Christianity possesses more symbols than any other religious faith. Crosses and creches, doves and ships, triangles and trefoils, grapes and wheat, lilies and luckinbooths—in Christianity, everything seems to have some deeper meaning beyond its outward appearance.

When one moves deeper into the Spirit, even things that have no apparent meaning begin to mean something. Every thing, every new moment, every breeze becomes filled with new meaning, grounded in the awareness that all of creation is pregnant with God. So it is with my favorite symbol of the Christian faith. This symbol has no widespread recognition or acceptance. People don't wear it as jewelry. They don't use it to adorn their churches or homes. It is never depicted in stained glass or engraved on church metal ware. As far as I know, I am the only one who sees it as a perfect symbol of the Christian life. Not surprisingly, I found it in my garden. My favorite symbol of the Christian life is the dandelion.

This sunny little flower is the true precursor of certain spring. Unlike crocus or robin which can arrive before the last snow or frost, it is a signal that surging life has begun and the ground is ready for the planting. Like the faith in many times and places, it is hunted and attacked with a vengeance by those who would rid their lives of its presence. However, like Christianity, it is resilient, refusing to be eradicated. Dig one out of your lawn and you find a deep root with many fine hairlike roots attached, just like the relationship of the Christian to the Lord of life. Since these hairlike roots break easily, you can never dig the entire plant out of the ground and, like Christians multiplying feverishly in the face of persecution, a new plant forms from the fragile root. "The blood of the martyrs is the seed of the Church," the old saying goes.

The most aggressive lawn lovers resort to chemical warfare to destroy the dandelion, like the despotic emperors of Rome whose determination to rid the empire of Christians was exceeded only by their unremitting cruelty. The lawn lover saturates his lawn with herbicide which will leech off their yards into the watershed, eventually poisoning the water they drink and in which their children bathe. And yet the dandelion will not be denied. Once its sun-like blossom fades, it is transformed in a little resurrection, becoming a wonderful puff ball of brilliant aerodynamic design, meant to carry the dandelion's genetic powerpack to waiting soil hundreds, thousands of yards away. Wasn't the Psalmist speaking of the dandelion hater when he wrote,

> He who sits in heaven laughs;
> the Lord has them in derision.

But the dandelion mirrors Christian faith in more than its tenacity. Like life in Christ, it is a nourishing thing, its leaves real food which carries more nourishment than the chemically pumped, plastic-wrapped produce which line the shelves of our supermarkets. When I was a boy, I would often see my father with a dandelion fork in his hand, scouring the backyard for a few young plants. Unlike our neighbors who would throw similar discoveries into the trash, I knew that these leaves were destined for a frying pan containing crumbled bacon, cracked pepper, and chopped water chestnuts, and that I would join him in a special meal of "Backyard on Toast." Like the faith, there is danger to be found in the dandelion as well as deep delight. For the wine that can be made from its leaves is often deceptively powerful, leaving those who have the courage to sample the fermented leaf astonished at its power to alter their perceptions and behaviors, just as Christ demands that we alter the way we see and act once we have drunk his blood and eaten his flesh.

Can anything compare to its beauty? Unlike the fussy rose which requires attention and assistance to come to flower or the bulb which becomes barren should its fragile blossom be picked by adoring hands, the dandelion sprinkles the unbroken expanse of common grass with prolific and resplendent color. Pick a flower, another quickly rises to take its place. Surrender to the joy of blowing its puff ball into the air and a hundred more will spring to life to delight your eye, nourish your body, and assert its dominance over the earth.

I have often wondered if horticulturalists have ever tried to refine the dandelion through the modification of root or leaf or blossom. Perhaps a strain of dandelion might be developed which has a broader and longer leaf for those who prize salads or make wine. There might even be a designer dandelion with a flower tinged with pink for those who long for some tonal diversity in their yard. Dandelions could be engineered to grow in difficult climates or only in attractive clusters so that the work of removing them from the garden would require attention to just a few spots instead of the entire lawn. Of course, the problem with manipulating the dandelion is that they would cease to be weeds and would, instead, be bred, cultivated beyond their original nature and habit. There would be "acceptable" and "unacceptable" dandelions, just as there are cultivated grapes and wild grapes, pampered strawberries and wild strawberries.

The church has often fallen into the trap of trying to redesign that which is best left wild. In the same way that flower and vegetable breeders develop rigid guidelines about what constitutes an authentic varietal strain, some families in the Body of Christ have established clear criteria about what kind of believer is doctrinally acceptable and which are outside their definition of discipleship. Unfortunately, this has led to a ubiquitous series of varietal definitions which, once established, have proven damnably difficult to overcome. Thus, congregations evolve which favor conservative Christians, or evangelical Christians, or charismatic Christians, or traditional Christians, or preservationist Christians. All of these congregations are glad to welcome new members, but often make it clear that welcome and conformity go hand in hand.

These acts of self-definition are certainly understandable in a society which increasingly depends on the study of consumer trends and target audiences for its economic vitality, but in embracing our culture's method of marketing we have become so refined, so focused that we have lost something essential about the nature of our religion. Christianity functions best when it is a wild-ranging, free-floating method of infection and influence. The unity of Christians is not found in our common liturgical or theological tastes, but in the unified nature of the wind which carries our seed, the Holy Spirit of God. Church leaders and administrators which attempt to specify conditions for blossom or leaf threaten to undo us, perhaps consigning us to varietal extinction. The more sophisticated and specific Christians become, the more we risk losing our purpose and mission to make the Gospel known to all nations, all sorts and conditions of women and men.

In recent years, the narrowing of the church has resulted in a variety of odious and tragic disputes. Many have attempted to keep the church in line with a past life shrouded in archaic and restrictive cultural practices, fearing that a deviation from tradition signifies a deviation from ecclesiastical efficacy. Others have promoted the abolition of all tradition, all rules in an attempt to pander to society, perhaps hoping to find an increase in acceptance by society at large. Both are guilty of a kind of restrictiveness. The former group restricts its understanding of the continuing revelation of

God to human beings. The latter restrict its understanding of success to the approval of the world around us. Both have lost sight of our primary purpose.

We are not now, nor have we ever been proponents of a particular cause or position. Like the dandelion, our purpose simply is to be what we are. In our case that means being alive in God, being sustained by God, and sending out the good news of life with God. We are to be as indiscriminate in our broadcast of good tidings as the dandelion is free with its seed. We are content to leave the sorting and naming and blaming to God. If our tastes or preferences in music or theology or liturgy conflict, we are to welcome those differences and give thanks for the incredible diversity of the family of faith.

Only when we have the courage to embrace our destiny as the world's wonderful weeds can we hope to grow into our heritage.

TWELVE

Some Days My Garden Smells Like Poop

I like words that are associated with the wind. "Breeze" is such a good word—a delight to say, evocative, almost kinesthetic. "Wafting" is another. "Zephyr." *Z*s and *f*s contribute to good wind words. They make a word so *tasty* somehow. "Blustery" is one that all A. A. Milne fans appreciate. Noisy words can be good wind words, like "rattling" or (especially at Halloween) "howling." "Whispering"—a delight to say, like imitating wind through aspens.

Despite the fact that no one enjoys it, the word that best describes wind in my garden is *poop*. The septic system at the rectory is at least as old as the house itself, and less than a model of superior sanitation engineering. As a result, when the wind kicks up, when zephyrs waft, they carry more than the scent of spring.

Smells are ever present in my garden. I stand in the center of the yard and allow myself the time to *breathe* my garden, to collect the aromas of work and growth and soil. I don't have to wait or search, for each new breath carries evidence of something near and some things far. A lavender rose called *Intrigue* with a perfume-like citrus. My pile of grass clippings, destined for the compost bin, smells like the old elephant house at the Philadelphia Zoo. The sharp odor of my tomato plants. A whiff of car exhaust from the bordering road. The thick and musty smell of emerging broccoli. And, of course, poop.

Other smells demand intimacy, insisting that I move close so that it may share its essence with me. The light peppery scent of dianthus. The clean but forbidding smell of French marigolds. The come-hither sweetness of phlox. Pungent leeks.

Surprisingly, some things have no scent at all, at least none I can perceive. My eggplant smell like nothing. The hot cherry and sweet bell peppers, despite their considerable impact on the tongue, are remarkably devoid of aroma. Pole beans bear only a generic green scent and my anemones, in contrast to their beauty, contribute nothing to the air around me. They are not alone. A hardy crepe myrtle with electric pink fronds, massive sunflower heads, titanic poppies, shaggy zinnias, cascading bleeding heart, black-eyed Susan—these, it seems, were made for the eye alone.

I close my eyes and imagine myself embraced by ever moving whirls of aroma, wrapping around me like the tendrils of a vine, each separate scent running across my face, infecting every breath with its own remarkable signature, and with old Democritus, I laugh out loud.

The Holy Spirit is such a place.

Many people find it difficult to think of the Holy Spirit in any but the most rudimentary terms. Some find it easy to imagine an overarching creator God who hovers over the cosmos, directing the vagaries of life. Others are able to look at Jesus and see the human face of God, but how are we to understand the Holy Spirit, the immanent, immediate, expressive experience of God in human life?

Once I became a gardener, I began to think of the Holy Spirit as the "windy" face of God. This was not a new revelation. Millennia before I set spade to earth, men and women of faith equated the Spirit of God with wind or breath. Ancient Hebrews referred to God's Spirit as *ruach*, a beautifully breathy word that meant "wind." God's ruach was more than just a result of God's breathing, it had power of its own. It was the ruach of God that transformed clay into man, ruach which empowered patriarchs and prophets. The Greeks referred to the Spirit as *pneuma*, or air, like the air that fills and toughens the pneumatic tire on a bicycle or automobile. I had known these things for years, but once I started a garden I came closer to understanding.

Despite all we have been taught, the Holy Spirit is not ghostlike. Unlike phantoms or wraiths, the Holy Spirit is not that local, not that contained. We should have been taught from our earliest years that the Holy Spirit is more like air than any physical thing, real or imagined.

Air is food. The process of breathing oxygenates our blood, and it is that oxygen, that air-food, that our body craves. While we breathe, we live. When we stop, we die. Everything that lives depends on air as food. Even the fishes deep in the sea live only because they can capture the air present in the water in their gills.

Air is place. It supports the flight of birds and supersonic jets. It brings vitality and the potential for growth when it is mixed with compacted soil. It is the essential membrane which allows earth to be earth.

Air is active. No one sees the wind, but we all have seen things caught in the wind. We have watched leaves or dust or sand or water soar from off the face of the earth and give itself to the wind. We have watched this flotsam leave one place and emerge somewhere else. There is no place or time when air is still. Even when we are caught in stillness and calm, the air still moves above us.

Air is connective. One of my earliest memories is of sitting at the living room window, listening for the sound of my father's whistling as he returned from work. We speak or sing or cry, but it is air which carries the sounds of our hearts to those around us. The air carries the music of life—warnings of danger, sounds of welcome, the protest of rage, the laughter of children.

This is the Holy Spirit—the ever-present, all-engulfing, nourishing atmosphere in which we live. Just as air provides space and substance for life, so the Holy Spirit is the life source of all energy, the vital element in all that exists. Just as air provides the atmosphere in which we move with ease, whether by foot, by car or by plane, so the Holy Spirit is a place of such breadth and depth that we can move remarkable distances in this same Spirit. This movement requires some time and practice, but once begun, those in the Spirit find that they are present to friends and loved ones thousands of miles away or many years departed, like Internet surfers who click from nation to nation on the World Wide Web.

Just as air is food for the body, the Spirit is food for the heart, providing encouragement, compassionate company, and constant invitation to holiness of life to those who would yield to the Spirit's longing.

However, while humans cannot live without air, it is possible to live in the world without living in the Spirit. Millions have succeeded in doing so. By sealing themselves off to any spirit but their own, they isolate themselves from growth and nurture and care. They are easily recognizable—miserable people living tragic or cruel lives, struggling to get by with a withered heart. These, like the seeds I plant that never germinate, like a cypress tree on a windy coast which is stunted, twisted by gale and surf never to achieve its potential, these are easy to spot and far too numerous.

I have often maintained that the purpose of the Christian church is not to get souls into heaven (after all, Jesus tells us that God will take care of that), but to get souls into the Holy Spirit, here and now, for the Spirit is the medium, like rich aerated soil, in which growth can occur.

Once in the Spirit, moving with delight in the windy heart of God, we are unlikely to leave. Like the smells of life, carried on the wind, the Spirit provides an atmosphere of indescribable spiritual fragrance. I stand in my garden, surrounded by the aroma of growth, knowing that the true breeze which enlivens and sustains me is nothing less than the breath of God.

THIRTEEN
On Felling a Tree

The cedar spits shards of rage as I press the bar of the chainsaw deeper into its flesh. Stinging my face and arms, the wood chips which fly from the trunk bring a curious sensation of pain and pleasure. I have reached the heartwood, and the tree, like a dying man, exhales, filling the air with cedar smell. Suddenly, I am seven or eight, exploring a deep under stairs walk-in closet by the light of a single bulb. The walls of the closet are lined with a dark red wood which exudes an odor I find nowhere else. The closet is in my grandparents' home, containing all the "winter things" of the household—blankets, woolens, great wintry overcoats. Despite the warmth of the July morning, I find some pleasure in their weight, their scratchy promise of comfort in months yet to come. The closet is not a gateway to an imagined Narnia but rather a treasure trove of genuine delights, for while the woollies occupy the first half of the closet, the second half is filled with the residue of my grandparents' former loves. As I have done a dozen times before, I open small metal boxes filled with fishing flies and run my finger across their fuzzy hairs and wings. I can name them all, and love the names themselves almost as much at these agents of deception—Royal Coachman, Gray's Nymph, Flying Ant. On one visit, my grandfather opened the closet to get a few folding chairs and found me looking through his collection. "What are they taking?" he asked, but I did not understand the question for another fifteen years.

Beyond the cane rods, fly boxes and wicker creels sits a machine of infinite complexity, no bigger than a breadbox but capable of transporting the family to other times and other places—an ancient Kodak eight-millimeter movie projector. Beside it are stacks of film cans containing a visual record of the family's life from black and white movies of my mother's childhood to faded color images of visiting grandchildren. I know that a small piece of my life is contained in one or two of those cans and they speak to my place in The Family.

Then there is the safe. A deep and imposing green with faded gold leaf scrolls for decoration, the safe is never locked. This is the holy of holies in the closet, a place of both promise and pain. I pull the heavy door open to see what I have seen many times: a stack of papers with an unloaded revolver holding them in place, a gold pocket watch in a graying chamois pouch, tray after tray of canceled checks, a pair of gold cuff links in a small brown paper envelope and, at the back, my box. The box is small, square, yet has a deep and satisfying weight when I lift it from the shelf. Inside the box are perhaps two dozen commemorative half dollars which my grandfather has culled from pocket change over three or four decades. He has told me that they will be mine when he dies, and that I am free to look at them each time I visit as long as I do not touch the revolver. As I inspect them one by one, I am caught between the desire to possess them and the fear of my grandfather's departure.

I once suggested, with the kind of presumption that only children bear, that it would be possible for me to enjoy them now, and that such an arrangement might completely forego the necessity of his death. Being a grandfather, he brought kindness and not judgement to my request. "Everything dies, Doug. Everything. Birds, trees, people. I will die someday, and your mother and father will die, and you will, too. It's just a matter of time." Like Saint Peter who, upon hearing the bad news protested, "No Lord, not that!" I challenged my grandfather out of love. "I don't want you to die!"

He was not a theologian; he was an economist, a specialist with numbers. Numerically trained, he responded the best he could. "If people didn't die, the earth would fill up pretty fast. Think how crowded the world would be!" While a crowded earth seemed a fair tradeoff for the continuance of my grandfather's life, I am afraid that the sting of desire for the half dollars kept me quiet.

Now I am in a crowded place and, unable to wait for time to act, I have put blade to bark to end a life born decades before. My victim is a white cedar which, shaded by other trees in the garden, sports growth only on its topmost branches, like a skinny man wearing a bad toupee. Aside from the stunted growth caused by the encroachment of its neighbors, it has another drawback. What foliage it has effectively prevents the sunlight from entering my home. As if planted by Druids, its trunk follows a perfect line of the sun's movement in the sky for three seasons of the year. My wife and I are both saddened by the decision, but we have come to the conclusion that it's time for the cedar to go.

Felling a tree is a solemn task. Loggers who harvest the forests for pulp must not feel what I feel, for I feel convicted by a decision to end a life. To be sure, that life does not have the value of human or animal life in my economy, but it is life nonetheless. He who cuts bears responsibility not only for surrounding growth, but for lives that may find shelter in its arms. My consolation is that nothing of this tree will go to waste. The branches and foliage will be chipped for mulch, the trunk cut to woodstove length.

The day is hot and the sawdust clings to my face, arms, and neck. The trunk is cut cleanly and quickly, falling in the exact spot I planned. Now the real work begins. Each branch is cut from the trunk, each frond torn from the branch. The trunk has to be rolled to give access to the underside. I yank repeatedly at the rope pull on the chipper until it roars to life, its pyramidal yaw hungry for action. It takes two hours of snapping branches and cutting crooked limbs, pushing and shoving still green boughs into the chipper. At the end, I have a small mountain of shredded tree, ready to spread around columbine and astilbe.

The trunk takes longer because I have determined to do more than make firewood. Almost as an act of penance, I take the two topmost sections of the trunk where I have intentionally left stubs of branches an inch long and bore wide holes in the wood. In winter months I will pack suet and peanut butter balls frosted with black oil sunflower seed into the holes for the chickadees, juncos and titmice. The only thing missing is a brass plaque: *This feeder is hung in loving memory of a once noble tree.*

I pause to wipe the sweat from my eyes, remove prickly branches from inside my shirt and realize that the act of felling a tree is momentous. The decision, the work required by the act itself, the smell of cut wood, the memories of past evoked, the resulting sun which streams into the windows of my house—all of these create a new reality: a new atmosphere in my garden and home, a new and profound respect for the dignity of what once stood, a sense of honor for the sanctity of memory. Yet, there is no doubt. The place is better without the tree.

Christianity, as it is expressed and practiced through the institutional church, suddenly seems much like my yard. It is graced with an ancient and vigorous liturgy which transports its members in some unexplainable way to a feeling of connectedness with the early church, even with Jesus himself. These towering ecclesiastical trees, like the 60-foot black walnut at the farthest part of my lawn, remain a prominent and indispensable part of our faith. They endure through the centuries because they continue to provide a constantly satisfying vehicle to lives and places which now exist outside of time. Communion, baptism, marriage, absolution, confirmation, ordination, unction—these, like mighty trees, continue to speak to the deepest needs of human longing.

Many churches refer to these acts as *sacraments*, a word which carries no meaning for most people living in the latter half of the twentieth century. Consequently, we describe these acts of faith and worship in terms of our own experience. "I was deeply moved at that wedding," some will say, or, "I found myself crying during Communion." These are emotional expressions of a greater truth: just as the tree shades my house, sacraments have a genuine impact on human beings, an impact which in many cases defies description.

Why is this so? Is it simply the result of the beauty and solemnity of liturgical pageantry? The impact of stirring or evocative music? The power of simple truths preached? Certainly, all of these contribute to the atmosphere of a sacrament, but there must be something more—some *connective reality* which allows these acts to take us back in time to tender or painful places or root us in the present moment.

One of the old trees that the church must dare to take down is the continued use of centuries old ways of describing and proscribing and initiating spirituality in worship. The church has built a barrier—a thorny hedge—around access to the divine life which effectively excludes those who have no history in the church beyond the occasional service on Christmas Eve or Easter morning. It is perhaps the greatest condemnation of the Christian family that those who visit once or twice a year rarely come back. Yet, had the liturgy been vibrant, vital, life giving, immediate they couldn't help but return week after week. As if it were under siege, the church perpetuates its own inadequacy in the vain hope that what has come before can be preserved for tomorrow. It would seem that we have forgotten the sacramental nature of sacraments—the fact that it is God's presence and activity in sacramental moments which engage the human heart, not the way we encase those moments in ritual.

When I was a child, I loved getting a new pair of shoes. A trip to the shoe store was a major event, and while I often wound up with shoes that were two sizes too big ("...he'll need room to grow!"), I got to keep the shoe box. To me, a shoe box was more than a container, it was a method of transport to the places of my imagination. I would cut out pictures of buildings or landscapes and paste them on the inside walls of the box. I would scour the garden for twigs that looked like trees or flowers small enough to fit the scale of the design (forget-me-nots were a favorite), then cut a hole in the end of the shoe box and look at the world I had created. Whether I made a moonscape with rocks and a picture of earth in the background or a busy London street, each peep into the box was an experience of entering something other: *other* than my world of home and school, *other* than the experiences of friends returning from seashore vacations or Pocono summers.

This is the effect of sacraments—they transport us to a state of mind we rarely find in our culture, specifically, "life with God in it." Popular culture as expressed in movies, books, television and radio is rife with secularity, creating worlds completely devoid of anything holy. In schools, young people can study quantum physics or survey seventeenth-century Lithuanian literature, but they may not speak of God. In such a culture, sacraments have no meaning until they are engaged and embraced.

A sacrament is simply an event where God reveals Godself to people. To be sure, this doesn't happen often in the movies or newspapers or on television, but the experience of people in the church is that it *always* happens when we enter into the Lord's Supper or when we wash in baptism, or when we celebrate the solemn vows exchanged by bride and groom. This is a remarkably interactive experience. God invites us into engagement, we respond, God *transforms* and *empowers* us through these acts. This is the holy place of meeting, of our enjoyment of God, and it happens hundreds of thousands of times every week, all over the world.

To be sure, there are some who are unaware of the hungry heart of God during these events. Perhaps their "God-eye" has not been sufficiently tuned to recognize the Holy One. But the testimony of others, 2,000 years worth of others, is that in these moments, God is always present and active.

My own experience is that sacramental worship does two things. It takes me back and brings me forward. In the same way that the smell of cedar transported me to my grandparents' closet (a memory as real and tactile as sunburn on my face), sacramental actions make it possible for me to move easily through time. However, while my memory (and the sounds and smells that evoke them) confines me to my own remembered history, my engagement with God takes me out of myself and places me squarely in God's remembering. Thus, through simple food of bread and wine, I am at table with Jesus himself. Through sprinkling of plain water on infant life I am at the Jordan as the heavens open. When forgiveness is begged and granted I become the woman, caught, who kneels at Jesus' feet.

Just as sacraments have the power to take me back, they also demand my attention to the present moment. Just as I must be attentive to the saw which cuts the tree (or face disastrous consequences), just as I must take care to insure the safety of living things in and around the felling site, so sacraments draw me to exquisite sensitivity of the moment. While talking about God in terms of time seems difficult if not impossible, we can comfortably say that God does not exist in the past nor in the present. Rather, God is always in the *now*. To be sure, we have the memory of God's mighty acts in ages passed, but sacraments are not a reliving of past moments. Instead, through the vehicle of sacramental action, God brings the essence of God's mighty work into our present moment. Unfortunately, far too many Christians keep looking back for answers to difficult problems or looking forward to possibilities. Most never realize that the embrace of humans and their God can only take place in the present moment where we receive from God the wealth of the ages in a way that we can act upon faithfully.

This is not a solitary experience. I may sit or kneel, basking in God's glorious presence, but cannot ignore the person beside me or behind me, who stand with me in the arena of God's activity. There are those I cannot see who define this meeting—homeless, hungry, wounded, poor, imprisoned folks who have God's compassion just as they did the ministration of Jesus.

Unfortunately, the church often restricts access to these holy moments to those who need them most. "You have to be a member here," or "you have to be a contributor," or worse, "we value you as a person but cannot approve of your choices," as though anyone present who fit their qualifications actually deserved by the quality of their life a face-to-face encounter with God.

This attitude of exclusivity is an old tree that the Church must cut down if it is to spread the experience of Good News among God's people.

And I, hard as it is to admit, have some old growth crowding out God's love in my own life. In time, the cedar will be mulch and food and warmth and I will turn to the inner trees which need to be felled.

FOURTEEN

Seeds of Change

The middle of February is a dreary time in the Philadelphia area. Neighbors to the far north still enjoy fresh blankets of snow, neighbors to the south taste the promise of spring's arrival. Philadelphia is wet, dank, gray. What snow remains is found in random little piles, blackened with grime and cinder. January's snowmen are but puddles on the lawn, and the favorite slope of young sledders has become nothing more than a mud lane. Baseball is six weeks away, snowdrops at least four. This is a nether-time, a time between times which most people simply endure, waiting for more light in the day and warmer air to draw them outside. It is in this time that my expectation builds.

The Burpee catalogue is usually the first to arrive. It sits in my stack of mail as thick as *TV Guide* with pages twice as big. Others follow quickly. The Cook's Garden, Thompson Seeds, Jackson and Perkins, Spring Hill Nurseries. I cull the catalogues out of the family mail and, like a man who has a map for buried treasure, quickly spirit them away to a secure place in my study for fear that some unthinking member of my family might discard one, counting it junk mail.

A dozen catalogues arrive within a week and I look for quiet times when I can riffle through their pages like a potentate who runs his fingers through his jewels. Every picture is of perfect flowers, perfect fruit, perfect vegetables, grown no doubt in The Land Without Aphids. Each description of habit, size, and productivity convinces me that my little square of soil could become a veritable Eden, bursting with life's infinite variety. Surely, with the power of these seeds and a herculean dedication to my garden I could feed the world. Not that I would grow everything available. The hungry of the world can do without kohlrabi. So can I.

Knowing that gardeners are multifaceted people, the catalogues all carry a complement of tools and accessories. I devour the descriptions of these as well. The Perfect Trowel. Nine different composting systems. Pike like tempered steel stakes for my soon-to-be nine-foot tomato vines. The Ideal Backyard Greenhouse (oh, how cruel to place it almost within reach!).

Despite the longing to accessorize, it is the seeds themselves which captivate me and claim my attention. I make the mistake of filling out the order form based on what I want to grow, not what my garden can sustain. Let's see—do I want an eighth of an ounce of wax beans or a quarter? Just how many seeds are there in an ounce, anyway? I sense that I have gone too far when I reach my second "additional page." A quick subtotal, and I find I have already hit the $300 mark. I start crossing things out—Turk's Turban squash, celeriac, lemon balm (we never really use it; I just like to crush the leaves between thumb and forefinger). I really want the bird bottle gourd, but perhaps I don't need four varieties of cantaloupe. All six strains of sunflowers stay, but the okra can definitely go.

Sitting in the comfort of my heated and dehumidified home, this process is primarily recreational. Selecting the seeds is fun, planting and growing them is fun, harvesting the produce is fun.

Seeds are perhaps the most remarkable of life's miracles: a tiny embryo surrounded by enough food to sustain its early life, packed in a protective case which, unaided, senses the proper time for the release of new life. Gauging warmth, moisture and external nutrient, the seed case yields to the atmosphere around it and loses its life so that the life within may emerge. I am neither a biologist nor a horticulturalist, so I am consigned to applying human attributes to these miraculous biological machines.

Seeds have real *power*. What other living thing has the capacity to increase its size by two or three thousand percent? The seed reproduces itself continuously, capable of making endless amounts of seed like itself.

Seeds are *patient*. I am told that seeds stored by Egyptians more than three thousand years ago still germinate and produce. A seed will wait for the perfect growing condition before it opens itself to the world around it.

Seeds are *dependent*. A seed can do nothing until the medium in which it planted reaches optimal condition. Until such time, the seed remains dormant.

Seeds are *self-sacrificing*. The seed must give up its existence if it is to achieve its potential.

Seeds vary in *quality*. Entire nations have endured famine because they had nothing but poor quality seed. What I do for pleasure, others around the world do simply to live. As I choose the contents of my garden and rush off a check, assured of quality seed, I am very much aware of those in other places for whom seed is not recreation, but a matter of life and death.

Add one more fact and the study of seed begins curiously to look like a sacrament: seeds do not germinate and grow until they are immersed in water.

Baptism is the act of seeding the garden of God. Like a workman whose knowledge of a certain tool increases with continued use, the church has increased in its understanding of the nature and purpose of baptism through the centuries. In earlier days, when infant mortality rates were higher and people feared that they could lose their salvation like a pocket possession, baptism was understood almost entirely in terms of saving power. Baptism brought the individual aboard a ship which tossed atop the flood of sin and immorality let loose on earth, insuring their safe arrival at some heavenly dock. Sometime later, it was seen primarily as the mark of membership in a supra natural body which transcended political and cultural boundaries—a kind of citizenship in a nation without borders. These interpretations (and others) found a certain validity in their times and continue to provide clues to baptism's greater meaning. Like roadside signs, they help point the way to a new depth of understanding.

Baptism is a ritualized action which allows us to act in response to something we already know; that there are interactive moments between God and human beings. Like a video game in which the player must actively participate to win, baptism is something that God and people do *together*. In looking at seeds, we can confirm some of the church's current understanding of the nature of baptism.

First, baptism has *power*. Just as the seed can grow to thousands of times its volume, baptism affords the individual the ability to become more than any human might imagine. The source of this power is a nontangible link between the person baptized and God. To be sure, many who are baptized never avail themselves of this power, but more often than not the individual baptized in Christ finds it difficult to ignore the constant pleading of God to draw nearer, drink of God's grace more deeply and grow into a life which is marked by compassion and action. All of this happens because baptism is a vehicle for transformation. Baptism actually changes things—it establishes a relationship between the person being baptized and God, a relationship which must either be pursued or ignored. Does this sound supernatural? Quite the contrary—it is very natural, and we see its earthly reflection in nature every day. The seed is saturated with water. It is transformed through germination and growth, or it simply becomes soggy and dies. Because baptism is interactive by nature, its full effect can only be realized when the individual makes the effort to grow. God's participation is remarkable: no matter how often the individual turns away from growth, God is always hungry for their return, always ready with sustenance and life.

Second, baptism is *patient*. No one coming from the font leaves in full flower. Like the seed which produces tree or vine, time and steady nourishment are required for the full realization of its potential. A baptized person may take years to develop into a full and fruitful vessel of God's activity, but God is willing to wait. Certainly, many who leave baptism never develop into much of anything spiritually. That, however, is not the fault of the sacrament, but rather the lack of nourishment provided to the seedling. In the parable of the sower and the seed, Jesus points out that there will always be those who make a good start, but will wither and die because they have no root. How many families have their children baptized because it is 'the right thing to do,' but absent them from the community's worship (or worse, neglect to institute family worship), only to bring them back for confirmation or marriage? Can anything, watered twice in a lifetime, live?

The painful truth is that baptism is *dependent*. Baptism has no value as an isolated act of social convention. It should never be offered or received unless those being baptized or presenting one for baptism long to engage the Holy One. Yes, God gives because it is God's nature to give, but unless the gift is unwrapped and used, it is meaningless to those who participate. Yet (and here is the paradox), the action of God in baptism is of inestimable benefit. Even if the effect on the individual is nothing more than a vague haunting that arises out of some long past sacramental action, baptism forges an inseparable link with God. Does God love or care for the person baptized more than the unbaptized? Certainly not! But baptism imposes a certain character of relationship between God and humans. In my tradition, the celebrant at a baptism pronounces surprisingly unequivocal words: "You are sealed by the Holy Spirit in baptism and marked as Christ's own forever!" Whether we yield or whether we rebel, baptism means that we are owned.

By its very nature, baptism assumes *self-sacrifice*. Jesus said that unless a seed planted in the ground dies, no fruit will emerge. It is important, however, to realize that being baptized does not demand that we give up ourselves. Rather, we strive to renounce those things which prevent us from becoming what we were intended to be. Like a rose that is decimated by Japanese beetles, never producing the full beauty of its flower, men and women are constantly assailed by corrosive forces which would prevent us from being fully human. To embrace our baptismal vows completely is to name and denounce those powers in life whose only aim is to consume us, leaving us mere shadows of human potential.

Some of the older theories about the meaning of baptism still carry weight and importance, albeit with a slightly altered view. As the sacrament was once seen as an initiation into a body of both terrestrial and cosmic proportions, so too we see baptism as initiation. However, we have come to understand that the act of baptism not only makes the individual a member of the church, but actually grafts one into Christ's own Body. Paul proclaims, "If anyone is in Christ, he is a new creation!" Like a tree prepared for a grafted branch, ready to feed and grow, we are branches in Christ, sacramentally (if not surgically) attached to a life-giving tree of incredible girth.

All of this begins when we, like the seed, are immersed in water. In God's economy, water is always the agent of change. The Flood, the crossing of the Red Sea, the waters of Meribah, the transformation of Jonah, the healing of the blind man in the pool of Siloam—ours is a *wet gospel*, a message pregnant with good news about immersion and washing and buoyancy.

Genesis tells us that the Spirit of God moved across the face of the waters at creation, urging latent life to grow, to become the jewel of the universe. Each time a soul moves to the font, the Spirit hovers once more.

FIFTEEN
Planting Things I Never Eat

I love to watch zucchini grow. First there is the flower—a star-shaped explosion of brilliant orange which opens itself generously to the bees who emerge from the depths of the blossom fairly covered with golden dust. When the flower wilts, the squash becomes visible beneath its shade. Small, light green, still clinging to the faded blossom at its tip, it looks like a wildly improbable nose on a circus clown. The growing then begins in earnest. First it is the size of a pencil, then of a blackjack, and unless it is harvested quickly, it more closely resembles a child's play zeppelin with a dark green, almost black, skin. The plant requires careful watching, as each dome-like mound of scratchy leaves can shelter five or six zucchini at any one time, all in varying stages of growth. On occasion I'll miss one's progress and find a mammoth squash hidden under a tangle of leaves. Two feet long. Four or five pounds. Overcome with excitement, I rush it to the kitchen where my wife passes judgement. "It's too big," she'll say. "It will be woody inside. I'll have to stuff it with rice and tender vegetables." Deflated, I beg her admiration. "But isn't it magnificent?" "Yes, dear," she smiles tolerantly. "Put it over there."

My early zucchini arrive about the third week of June. These small *courgettes*, as the English call them, are sweet, tender (almost liquid when steamed) with a thin and flavorful skin. We easily devour the first dozen. By the second week of July, I am bringing four or five zucchini into the kitchen each day where they are placed next to yesterday's harvest, which sits next to the produce from the day before. Mealtimes become less like a symphony and more like variations on a theme—steamed zucchini, fried zucchini, zucchini medley, stuffed zucchini. I know our stockpile has reached a critical mass when I return home from work to find rows of cooling zucchini bread sitting on wire racks, destined for the freezer and enjoyment in less temperate times. Still, the freezer is only so big.

I initiate a surprise for friends and coworkers. "Look," I say, as if I were bestowing the Nobel Prize, "I've brought you zucchini from my garden!" Quite

57

a few folks blanch, some open canvas bags to show me the squash they were hoping to unload on me, others simply avoid me for the rest of the summer.

Last year I bought a six-cell flat of cherry tomatoes called "100s and 100s." They lied. When the fruit started to set, I realized that it should be named "1,000s and 1,000s." I started to harvest the quarter-sized fruits in mid-July. Soon after, the plants sported perfect fruit in the evening that had not been ripe earlier in the day. Every day brought another three or four dozen cherry tomatoes to our kitchen. I began to feel like Lucille Ball, stuffing chocolates in her mouth when the conveyor belt went awry. I started passing out gallon sized plastic bags full of them to those who had somehow missed the joy of my zucchini.

Green beans. Italian flat beans. Wax beans. Lima beans. Despite careful succession planting, they all come in at once like a woman in labor who cannot stop the body's urgency to produce. Keep three or four quarts, give eight or nine quarts away.

Some of my vegetables never make it to the gift stage. There is never enough eggplant to satisfy my family's desire. Every leek is prized, admired for its stoutness and girth and promptly transformed into vichyssoise or leek and sausage quiche. I have never had much luck with onions, but try a different strain every year in hopes of finding the right one. They never reach the level of bounty I hope for, but there are always ten to fifteen that are keepers. All the garlic is kept.

Then there are the potatoes. I love growing potatoes for two reasons. First, they require finesse in the harvest demanding a certain amount of patience on the gardener's part. Dig them too soon and you have nothing but a handful of little potato pebbles. Harvest them too late and the skin is tough, the flesh indistinguishable from store bought. Second, there is little that can compare to the joy of digging and discovering—finding that the earth has hidden treasures just inches beneath its surface.

I usually plant two types of potato—a russet and a golden. Each has its own perfect harvest time. The russets are ready earlier, and I scrape away the soil at the base of the plant, finding exciting flashes of neon pink skin and feeling much like the man who found a pearl of great price buried in a field. These little jewels are smaller than a baseball; they could grow larger, but who could bear to miss the taste and texture of new potatoes boiled with salt and butter, or new potatoes browned in olive oil and garlic?

The goldens seem perfect to me about a month later. These are the large, firm fleshed potatoes that are destined to be baked or mashed or fried. Unlike the russets, they are remarkably easy to find as they tend to grow in a circular crown just below the surface of the earth. The russets can grow as deep as a foot or two beyond the base of the plant, creating a sense of earnest exploration at harvest lest one or two be neglected. Invariably I miss a few, not to be found until late fall when I till my shredded leaves and grass clippings deep into the soil in preparation for next year's garden.

There is something about distributing potatoes to friends that compels the grower to exercise some caution. Admittedly, they could be stored for quite a while, but only at the moment of harvest are they perfect, creamy in consistency. There are always more than we can eat, but the gift packs are distributed with judicious care, destined only for those who can truly appreciate them.

As much as planting, weeding, tending and harvesting, gardening is about the distribution of wealth. Gardening is taking the richness of creation and spreading it around. The accomplishment of this ideal, however, takes some imagination. Not everyone wants what I have to offer, so I must search for those who need what I have to give. In the past, I have set up a "Harvest Pew" at the back of the church during summer months. Members of the congregation who live in apartments and have no garden of their own take what they want. My contributions are supplemented by other gardeners who find themselves overloaded with produce, and the church begins to look like a greengrocery. An area organization which distributes fresh food to homeless shelters picks up many of our vegetables weekly, delivering to men, women, and children who may not be able to even imagine having land to till. At times our produce feeds the family who find themselves caught between the next week's paycheck and an empty cupboard.

Imagine how dull it would be to plant a garden and not be able to share it! I must admit to deep and satisfying pleasure whenever someone says, "Ooo-your potatoes were wonderful!" If I were honest, I would have to admit that my garden produced a lot that wasn't edible.

I have just come in from weeding the garden on an unseasonably hot June morning. Much to my dismay, I have found that there are more species of weeds in my little space than there are types of vegetables. There are light green leafy things that look like lemon balm but have the odor of red ants. There's a star burst-shaped fleshy weed that lies flat on the ground and looks like portulaca, but bears no flower. There is a little bushy weed that looks like a bundle of shamrocks and sets a tiny yellow flower. I tend to like this best of all my weeds because it yields so easily when I pull it. Crabgrass is ever present as are those flat broadleaf things with the seedy spike. Chickweed, of course, and lots of vining weeds that twine and choke faster than I can pull. All of these compete for air, light, nutrient, determined to dwarf that which I have planted.

Over the years, I have learned a few things about weeding. First, weeds are easier to eliminate if the ground has been well prepared and respected. After tilling in the spring, my soil is loose and friable. I am careful not to walk within a foot or two of my planting so as to keep the soil light. Consequently, weeds are more easily pulled as their roots have not become an integral part of the soil's structure. Second, chemicals may be a quick fix, but have little long-term benefit. Third, mulching heavily inhibits weed growth. Fourth, there are some good times to weed and some bad times: weeding is almost a pleasure after a steady rain, while weeding in a drought is tortuous.

The human spirit produces abundantly. Its growth bears a remarkable resemblance to the garden. In the same way that I have never had luck with cantaloupe but excel in the production of zucchini, we all have areas of spiritual proficiency and spiritual weakness. Some of these areas of spiritual skill (like growing zucchini) are relatively common, and can be accomplished by almost anyone. Others require years of discipline and effort before they come to fruition and are rare and precious when they are found. In the same way I admire the master rose grower who hybridizes with apparent ease, so we look with deep appreciation at the spiritual master who has tuned their inner life with a high degree of success. Like gardeners with an abundance of food, these are the ones who provide the greatest spiritual offerings to enrich our own humble attempts at inner health. Saints, we call them. There is something almost timeless about the quality of the insight and direction they have to offer. Of course, these special saints of God are at something of a disadvantage in the way we approach them. Popular thinking over the years has cast these spiritual giants as something other than what we know ourselves to be. Their insights were so keen, so on target that we tend to assume that they must be on a different level than "ordinary" folks.

Nothing could be further from the truth. Many of these spectacular saints were spectacular sinners as well or were encrusted with quirks and idiosyncracies. Francis of Assisi stole from his father's business. One of Saint Augustine of Hippo's favorite hobbies as a young man was heckling Christian preachers. Saint Julian of Norwich was absolutely dotty about cats (although a large portion of the population would hardly consider this odd!). Thomas Cranmer renounced his faith under pressure. Saint James and Saint John, the only team of brothers among the original disciples, were so hot tempered that Jesus nicknamed them *Boanerges*, "sons of thunder." William Laud was rigid in doctrine and politics. Saint Isaac of Syria was probably a manic depressive. These aren't alone. The great saints of God were at times intolerant, stiff necked, myopic, and argumentative: quite a "weedy" collection of people. But, they were also productive. Amazingly, they never let their sin stand in the way of their sainthood. They themselves determined that in spite of their flaws, they would offer what gifts they had. We, on the other hand, frequently allow our sinfulness to obscure our saintliness. I have spoken with people about their faith for 25 years, and I have found that, as Pogo said, "we have met the enemy and they is us." We have somehow convinced ourselves that the gifts with which we have been endowed are of little value. Further, we believe that even if we have something of value to offer another, it is desperately outweighed by our insufficiency. Imagine a gardener saying to a hungry child, "Well, I have some tomatoes and peppers and squash here, but you probably won't want them because I have some bad personal habits!"

People also seem convinced that their spiritual giftedness is not worth offering because it can't be compared to the insight and skill of those who have gone before them in faith. The apostles knew this feeling. Once, when Jesus had spent a day teaching a large group of people, those present became hungry. Jesus asked the disciples to find out what food was available. "Well," they hemmed, "there's a boy here with five loaves and two fishes, but that's certainly not enough!" Filled with inadequacy, the apostles had decided to make Jesus' mind up for him! I wish I had a photograph of their faces when all were fed out of a simple gift and there were leftovers to spare!

So often we, discounting our abilities, try to make Jesus' mind up for him, certain that he can do nothing with that which he has given us. If there is a single greatest sin in the latter half of the twentieth century, it is this— that the people of God have effectively hidden their light under industrial strength bushel baskets, certain that the light would only hurt someone else's eyes. Think with what light we might have flooded the world if we had been convinced that God was more interested in working with our little strengths than condemning our great weaknesses.

That's the trouble, isn't it? We find ourselves in weedy gardens and are certain that the abundance of weeds reduces the value of the fruit. Here again, the garden provides insight into our need. *Well-prepared soil makes weeding easier.* The individual spirit which is tended to regularly, molding and shaping itself into Christ becomes a place where sin finds it difficult to set deep roots. As in gardening, vigilance is the key.

Millions of Americans begin the day by checking their weight, their pulse or blood pressure, the progress of their investments, the status of their workplace. If we are to remain healthy and fruitful, we must check our spiritual state as well. It used to be called a daily *examen*—the intentional act of reviewing the day and our actions in it, looking for roots which might undermine our ability to produce abundantly. Second, while special rigorous spiritual exercises or retreats and conferences (the chemical growth stimulants of spirituality) might provide a dramatic and intense emotional experience, the lifelong business of spirituality is not about mountaintop experiences, but rather it is seeking a long, steady, consistent pattern of living that can carry us through the deepest valleys. In the past, this commitment to daily spiritual effort was ritualized, providing a uniform regimen for a large number of people with diverse and extraordinary needs. "Say Morning and Evening Prayer daily," the church used to say, "using these readings from this lectionary, these canticles in regular rotation, adding these antiphons on first and second (but not third!) Class feasts. Do not neglect proscribed days of obligation and if you can't attend the Eucharist daily, make a spiritual communion." Whew! At one point in history, that language proscribing those actions may have made some sense to most people, but our age is one of liturgical illiteracy. Yet, as we can see from signs all around us, it is also a time of deep spiritual hunger. Unfortunately, since the church's suggestions are almost unintelligible, people turn to other, more easily understandable (if less efficacious) suggestions: "Bake your quartz crystal at 250 degrees to clear it of negative emotions, then coddle it in your hand while imagining your dearest desire." "Try to imagine your essence floating six feet above the ground connected to your seated body by a blue cord." "In a secluded place, scream from the depths of your body to release your primal emotions." Which is the least effective—a church which does not provide good tools for daily spiritual work, or fads which leave people feeling silly, or worse, a failure?

Ultimately, we must develop our own daily regimen, one which is capable of allowing us to enjoy the mountaintops while helping us endure the valleys. I cannot prescribe a specific regimen precisely because no one set of disciplines can meet every individual's need. I can, however, identify some of the major components of every good inner discipline.

There must be time to examine ourselves in order to discover where we are true to our own ideal and where we have departed from it. There must be time for actively engaging God in what the old hymn calls "mystic sweet communion." While those aren't the words which we would use to describe human lovemaking, that's about what they mean. They mean we must have time to enter into and enjoy God, and to experience God's enjoyment of us. There must be time for input from an irrefutable source. The Bible is my favorite irrefutable source, not because the Bible is infallible, as some would insist, but that despite its internal inconsistencies, it invariably points to God. There are other sources I cherish in addition to Scripture. Most of them are in books. Some are not, like music. I don't just mean sacred music, although I enjoy much of it. All sorts of music speaks to me about God, and, strange as it seems, the more I work to move closer to God, the more I find hints of God in all kinds of music, especially secular music.

Finally, there must be time for charging. While my daily discipline charges my spiritual batteries, here I mean a different kind of charging. I feel incomplete if I do not leave my discipline without a specific plan for the day. My date book carries one kind of plan—a plan for my time. My discipline leaves me with a behavioral plan to abandon some of my behaviors, and to work on strengthening others. It keeps my feet on the ground when I arrive at mountaintops. It lifts me up when I wander through valleys of deep shadow.

I have also found that there are good times to work on my spiritual weeds, and times that are not so good. In times of discouragement or sadness, the "drought" times of the soul, I am too weak to make a successful effort at wrestling with my sinfulness. My only desire is to endure. However, there are also times of strength and vigor within me when I can tackle my weaknesses more effectively.

I remember a conversation I had with a friend many years ago. My friend had been deeply troubled by a personal weakness and felt he wasn't making any progress in dealing with it. After a while, he felt better about himself, about his work, and about his relationship with his family. "It was the strangest thing," he said. "Here I was feeling really good about myself and I felt God say to me, 'I have some extra time if you would like to work on that weakness now.'" I'm sure that God always has time, but my friend was only able to make use of it when he felt strong enough to avail himself of God's willingness to help.

But be careful! There's something else I have learned about weeds—I like some of them! Some are attractive, like the shamrock-shaped weed with the pretty yellow flower. By the same token, I quite enjoy some of my sins. They feel good! These, I am afraid, are the most difficult to uproot and may require years of arduous work to eradicate them completely.

The idea, of course, is to produce as much fruit as possible while weeding out the weaknesses which hinder growth. Once the fruit is ripe, no matter how simple or common, our goal must be to give it away.

SIXTEEN
A Tale of Two Tomatoes

Many years ago, while serving a congregation in Long Island, I planted a garden. I didn't stay at that church for long, but it was long enough to create some raised beds and try the square foot method of gardening for a few years. My timber lined plots didn't sport a great variety of vegetables, just a few different kinds of tomato, some potatoes, leeks, onions, and lots of squash. Because the garden was small, it was also manageable and I fooled myself into thinking that I was quite the gardener. I had even begun to explore the pleasures of composting, taking leaves and grass clippings and other organic matter and piling them in a heap in a corner of the yard. Being more familiar with the name than the method, I never turned the pile, never watered it, never aerated it. As a result, it was more a pile of old dead junk than a compost heap, but it gave me pleasure to think I was doing something environmentally friendly with my leafy refuse.

Throughout the growing season I would fling all sorts of things onto the top of the heap—pulled weeds, spent stalks from faded sunflowers, grass clippings, fallen twigs and leaves. At the end of the season after the first killing frost I uprooted all the remaining plants in the garden and dumped them on top, having first stripped them of any young fruit that might mature in the cool and friendly confines of my basement. During the winter months, I would look out the window at the compost pile from the warmth of my home, finding deep satisfaction in the fact that the pile's internal temperature prevented snow from sticking. It was working. By spring I would have a mound of black gold.

April arrived, the time of bed preparation for cool crops—peas, lettuce, broccoli, and the like. Pitchfork in hand, I dug deep into my compost heap, looking for that crumbly dark humus I had so often seen in catalogues and gardening magazines. I lifted layer after layer, only to find that the organic trash I had dumped in the corner had been transformed not into soil enriching compost, but rather into wet, darkly colored organic trash. Here were the sunflower stalks, soft and wet, to be sure, but still sunflower stalks. Underneath were the spent pepper plants, the eggplant stalks with wilted leaves still attached, the flattened and sorrowful looking stems and leaves of the crooked neck squash. I had come to dig gold, but had found the leafy equivalent of a sodden newspaper instead.

Unwilling to plant without fortifying the soil, I bought those large plastic bags of peat and sanitized manure that seem so heavy when one carries them to the beds, but cover surprisingly little ground. Damn the compost. My soil would be rich without it.

It was a good year for gardening. There was regular and moderate rainfall, warm days and cool evenings. My plantings, expanded over the previous year's, grew luxuriantly. Especially impressive were the potatoes, a vegetable particularly fond of Long Island's soil and climate. Gratified, I turned my back to the ersatz compost heap, determined to succeed without it.

Sometime in mid-June, one of my daughters was playing in the backyard while I was cultivating my beds. She called out to me, "Daddy, what's growing in this garden?" Turning my head I saw she was standing next to the traitor compost pile. "That's not a garden, honey, it's just some old junk," I said, turning back to the soil. "But what's growing here?" she asked. I got up and walked down to the pile. Her little finger pointed to a dozen, perhaps two dozen little seedlings emerging from the mound. "What are you growing here, Daddy?" she asked.

Even though they were only four or five inches high, it was easy to identify them. "They're tomatoes, Claire."

"Did you plant them?"

"No, I didn't. They must have grown from the seeds of the rotted tomatoes I threw on the pile last year."

"Can we keep them?" she asked, filled with an excitement akin to that of a child who has just found a stray cat.

"Sure," I said in a 'why not?' tone. "We'll just let them grow there and see what happens. How's that?"

"Can this be my garden?"

"I suppose so."

"Do I have to do any work in it?"

"No," I said. "Just keep an eye on them. Watch them grow."

"That's the kind of garden I like," she said, and walked off to play on the swings. Me too, I thought.

All summer Claire kept an earnest vigil at the mound and each night at the dinner table, my wife and I would receive a detailed report of how many leaves her tomato plants had grown, how many blossoms had emerged, how high the spindly plants had stretched. On the day that the first flower fell revealing a tiny tomato bud in its star-shaped holder, the whole family was taken to the mound to oohh and ahhh over Claire's apparent success with things living. Before long there were a dozen or more tiny tomatoes and the dinner table reports were studded with the language of mathematics. Number one was half an inch across, number two almost an inch, number three ten inches off the ground.

Not surprisingly, when ripening time came, there was a marked difference between the tomatoes which enjoyed the tender affection I lavished on my beds and the stunted and misshapen tomatoes that struggled in the mound. Claire wasn't terribly disappointed. It was enough for her that we took her dwarfed fruit and chopped out the best bits, adding them to the sauce which would be simmered then frozen for the winter months. However, before the chopping we lined all our tomatoes up on the kitchen counter including the sad little products of the mound. Hoping to transmit some valuable botanical information, I asked Claire why some were big and some were small. "Because you loved the big ones."

I felt like a boxer had punched me in the chest. I was hoping to teach her something about gardening but she had seen something more fundamental and redirected my attention to a greater truth about life. The things I love flourish, the things I neglect fall far short of their potential.

My first response was to think of the thousands of throw away and neglected children who stud our landscape like withered vines. My mind and my heart quickly moved to the vast numbers of elderly people who are warehoused in care facilities that are content to maintain, rather than grow, their residents. I thought of our nation, so unloved that less than half the populace cannot find their way clear to vote in a general election. I thought of the church whose roles are burgeoning with names, but whose worship is attended only by a faithful few lovers.

Then, in a moment of true horror, I looked at myself. Like a computer screen which flashes the files and programs it contains in a split second of internal processing, I was able to name a dozen parts of myself that I have loved and encouraged to grow, a dozen more that I had abandoned to the mound of neglect. I wasn't terribly proud of the list.

There were times when I loved my anger more than my desire for peace and reconciliation. There were times when I loved my appetite more than the well being of my body. At other times, I loved my need for inactivity more than my wife's need for respite from the responsibility of children and home. My hunger to be liked and appreciated almost always grew larger than my dedication to truth and fairness. Even my love of God was at times obscured by my desire that God should want what I want, do what I want God to do. Certainly, there were some positives on the list, but as valuable as they were, they could not eradicate the effect of the "big tomatoes" which drove their dwarfed and more valuable counterparts toward relative obscurity in the garden of my inner life.

The work of naming the areas of care and nurture I had loved, along with those I had neglected, lasted for much of the following week. Toward the end of that week, I faced another, even more troubling, realization. As a priest and pastor responsible for several hundred souls, I had at times preached a gospel which made forgiving allowance for my own stuntedness.

Worse, I condemned those who weren't working on areas of their spirit that I had mastered in my own. What I deplored in others, I myself displayed—the message that I was OK, everyone else was so-so.

Nothing in life is as useless yet as comforting as a convenient gospel. In the same way that I had always been content to celebrate my strengths while turning a blind eye to my spiritual deficiencies, many of us come to the gospel looking for Jesus' sweet side while neglecting his radicality. We love his condemnation of the Pharisees, claiming him as our personal hero, but promptly forget the "log in our own eye." We love Jesus loving, but ignore his command to love one another *in the same way* he loved us. We thrill at the healing of the lame and halt, the blind and mute, but insist that his healing hand stop at the borders of our spirit lest he heal too much. If we marvel at his power to raise the dead, we do so only hoping that he does not interfere with the dead and dying spots within ourselves. 'Give me forgiveness,' we cry, 'like the forgiveness you gave to the woman caught in adultery, but spare me the responsibility.' Story after story, we come to Jesus longing for the comfortable, the easy parts of good news, hoping to remain unaltered by the challenging and transforming.

The gospel, with remarkably relative ease, can and is transformed every day by those who find some things attractive, others daunting. Like a gardener who sits down with a seed catalogue, saying yes to some varieties, no to others, we are too often guilty of creating a "pick and choose" gospel. I, I who was supposed to know better, I who was entrusted with the care of souls, I who claimed to be an advocate of the whole gospel of God, I, too, was guilty.

Winter was cold and hard that year in Long Island. Bitter temperatures and numerous heavy snows kept me in warm places with ample time to work on my spiritual fruit. I spent a long time with the gospel accounts, circling and underlining those passages that I believed I had glossed over. Like a gardener giving away vegetables both ripe and undeveloped, my prayer time became a lifting of my inadequacies into the presence of God while gratefully holding fast to those which were on their way toward maturity. Confession helped, not just to my wife and to friends who loved me no matter what, but to the same people and from the same pulpit where I had at times proclaimed a comfortable gospel.

When the icy grip of winter yielded to the promising breezes of early spring, I sat down with Claire. "I have an idea," I said. "Do you remember the tomato plants that grew out of the compost heap? Let's not buy any tomato plants this year—let's see if we can get our plants from the corner of the garden!" As I hoped, seedlings began to appear by early May and Claire and I gently transplanted them into our raised beds. The pleasure of transplanting was enhanced by the fact that we didn't really know what would grow. Would they be Big Boys, beefsteaks, plum tomatoes, cherry tomatoes? As it turned out, we had some of each and enjoyed a bumper crop of the most deeply satisfying fruit I had ever tasted.

SEVENTEEN

What to Do When Winter Comes

The snow has been falling for more than eight hours. It has already reached a depth of seven inches in open spaces, eighteen or more in places where it drifts. My daughters' schools have been closed for the day, and will probably be closed tomorrow as the weather services are predicting another three to five inches overnight. My children are overjoyed, running around the house singing the songs of the recently liberated. Our suggestions that they might use this time to clean their rooms or catch up on homework or read a good book are met with scorn and disbelief. "Mo-om," they whine, turning that simple name into a multisyllabic moan, "this is a free day! You don't do work on a free day, you just have a good time!" It's hard to argue, so the television is turned on, the video tapes are spread out like a new catch upon the shore and *The Princess Bride* plays for the 140th time in our home. The Monopoly board is set between the wood stove and the TV, and the arguments begin about the cost of hotels and the potential uses of the "free parking" space. It sounds and feels good to me.

My love of snowy days has kept me from considering employment in places south and west that are deprived of its gentle grace. "But you can drive to snow anytime you want," one Californian suggested. True, perhaps, but the character of the experience is different. Driving to the snow involves a certain *intentionality*: packing the kids and their entertainments into the car, enduring the drive, finding a place to play and, more importantly, a place to rest with plenty of bathrooms. Being *in* the snow requires no such effort. "Snow is God's way of saying that you are working too hard," I say to those who complain. Snow is enforced relaxation, at least until it is time to shovel.

As a gardener, I am grateful for the snow—for its blanket of protective warmth atop my flower and vegetable beds, for the slow and deep watering it provides the soil. Still, I am itchy on winter days.

I wander through the house checking the status of the potted plants. To my dismay, I find that they don't need my help. There are no weeds in the African violets, the philodendron isn't crowded, the Christmas cactus is doing fine. Aloe plants multiply without my assistance, spider plants thrive on neglect, the tradescantia needs nothing I have to offer.

The week before the storm, I walked through my backyard aimlessly, picking up fallen branches breaking them into kindling size, scraping up the few remaining leaves I had missed during fall cleanup. I stood wistfully at the border of my garden space remembering the crop that was planted here last summer, and the one the summer before. I had already planned next season's garden a dozen times, taking into account rotation and companion planting. Now there was nothing to do but wait. I know that winter brings specific delights, but skiing and tobogganing and hot buttered rum by the fire all seemed to me to be inward pleasures—the things we do to pass the time until we can engage the earth once more. It is the *interactivity* with the earth which delights me, which connects me to life outside myself.

Standing at the window watching the snow fall, I have to admit that any time of waiting and endurance is, for me, a winter time. These days of spiritual and emotional winter descend upon the human spirit from time to time in life, but unlike times of expectancy and excitement, like waiting for the birth of a child, a spiritual winter tends to be bleak and devoid of delight. The time between the loss of a job and accepting a new position—this is a winter time. The expanse of time from the moment your child becomes sick until the moment she is well again. This is winter time. Keeping vigil at the deathbed of a loved one—this, too, is winter time.

But there are other moments, even more frightening. For the individual who struggles to live in the Spirit of God, there are times when God seems nowhere near; cold and forbidding times when we call, but receive no answer.

Doubt isn't the problem. Doubt is an intellectual dilemma which has us question the points and principles of believing. Spiritual winter times are fueled by despair and discouragement. God no longer seems near, eager for our company and we begin to think that the moments of engagement we enjoyed in the past were simply the delusions of a hungry and gullible heart.

The Hebrew scriptures tell us that Israel endured two such times as a nation: the wandering of the children of Israel in the wilderness and the exile of the nation's brightest and best in Babylon. Both were characterized by despair and discouragement, yet despite the hardship and anguish of these two winter times, they remain the defining moments of biblical Judaism. The Gospel accounts mirror Israel's experience by placing Jesus' winter times at the beginning and end of his ministry. The stories of the temptation in the wilderness and Jesus' anguish in the garden of Gethsemane not only point to the life of Jesus as the embodiment of the life of Israel, they proclaim that no life lived to the fullest is lived without winter times. Some of those winter times are personal, some found in the arena of relationships, others in our careers. One of the most painful I can remember involved all three.

Five years into my work as rector of a large congregation I have run headlong into a seemingly immoveable wall of despair. A spirit of *malaise* has gripped the congregation I serve. Nothing I do seems to please anyone. Members of the congregation constantly complain about their dissatisfaction with my leadership. People talk about their affection for the former rectors, and their discontent with the current direction of our common ministry. When asked to be specific in identifying areas of concern or dissatisfaction, lay leaders respond only by saying that my personality is too strong or my style of ministry is alienating. Strangely, they say nothing about themselves, about their role in our common sojourn. There is ample evidence of sabotage: constant rumor mongering in the community, people talking behind my back, congregants criticizing my wife and children.

Believing that the problem may well be me, I take their criticism to heart, holding their anguish up against my life as a kind of template. It is obvious even at the outset that the two don't fit. My first reaction is to doubt the quality of my own leadership. Perhaps I'm not right for this congregation; worse, perhaps I'm not right for any congregation. Perhaps I shouldn't be in parish ministry at all. I begin to cast around for other visions—would I be better in law, in finance, in business? These, as well as every other possible mid-career change I can think of, I discard quickly. I cannot begin to imagine myself as anything other than a priest in the church of Jesus Christ. Yet, under the leadership of my priesthood, my people seem to be unhappy, their grumbling becoming epidemic. Nothing specific that I can identify seems to be wrong in this place. The Gospel is being proclaimed, works of compassion and care are being accomplished, the sick and infirm were being ministered to, the poor being visited and relieved in their distress. Despite all this, people are unhappy, and have made it clear that I am the source of their unhappiness. I resign myself to one of two possibilities. Either I am wrong about myself or they are wrong about me.

Like many other people I know, I am uncomfortable with conflict. There are some, to be sure, who find the assertion of their will and desire the most natural of all behaviors, but I am not one of them. I like people to be happy, living and working in peace. I realize that I also suffer from a fairly common fatal flaw—I like to be liked and want my work to be valued by those I work for. Both of these desires have set me up for disappointment. Perhaps these things exist in some other profession, I think. Surely, there's something out there I could do which wouldn't make me the butt of peoples' anger.

As soon as my escapist thoughts surface, I realize that I have entered into self-pity. Running away from the dissatisfaction of others isn't an escape from their problems or the satisfaction of their desire, it's an abandonment of the demands of the Gospel. My job isn't to be popular. It's to be faithful. I turn the problem again in my mind, examining it from different angles.

I am suddenly struck by how *personal* all of this seems. None of the issues which I can identify center on the exercise of our work or our mission as a church. Caught in the web of criticism, I have been damned by questions of personality rather than purpose. These people do not, it seems, want to be without leadership, they just want a different kind of leader; one who will lead them the way they want to be led to places they want to go.

I know how *intense* the situation is. The sabotage I experience isn't casual or random, it is focused and constant. It takes a tremendous amount of energy to sustain that kind of anger, energy usually reserved for times when something we cling to has been threatened.

Listening to parishioners who feel some distress led me to realize that the complaining is *unreasonable*, not that they don't have a right to their feelings, but that those feelings are beyond reasonable discussion. Some have placed an impenetrable wall of dissatisfaction around themselves, one impervious to discussion, negotiation, or compromise.

Wait a minute. I begin to feel the stirring of familiarity, of a story often told. "Why did you take us out of Egypt where we had cucumbers and melons and leeks, just to die out here in the wilderness?" That sounds familiar. "Why did you leave us for so long when you went up on the mountain?" Sounds personal to me. "Why have you brought us here only to be defeated by giants?"

With a flash of recognition and relief, I realize that it isn't me, and it isn't them, it's life. Life is filled with winter times, with wilderness experiences which bring anguish and uncertainty, and in the midst of those times people tend to feed on their leaders and on each other. Many things can be said about Israel's sojourn in the wilderness, but we must never romanticize the events of their winter time. Israel never moved joyfully and purposefully through the wilderness—they were dragged, kicking and screaming all the way. They never had confidence in their leadership, but fought against it constantly, kicking Moses at every turn. Even at the very brink of their destination they looked at the land of Canaan and wanted to run away. I begin to wonder if Moses wasn't secretly relieved when the Lord prevented him from crossing the border of the promised land, forcing Israel to go on without him.

If the diagnosis of my situation comes from the wilderness experience, I find my future direction in the Exile. About 650 years after Israel's entrance into Canaan, King Nebuchadnezzar of Babylon embarked on a military campaign that led to the defeat of Jerusalem and the enslavement of Judah's strongest young men and women. Taken far from their homes and family, they languished in their encampment in Babylon, enduring the misery of exile. The prophet Jeremiah, hearing of their distress, wrote them a remarkable letter on how to deal with winter times. "Build houses and live in them," he writes. "Plant gardens and eat what they produce. Take wives and have sons and daughters; take wives for your sons, and give your daughters in marriage, that they may have sons and daughters; multiply there and do not decrease." Set deep roots, rejoice in relationships, pray and work in the painful place.

I made the first of many gardens in that place that year, and shared the harvest with my congregation. I planted trees around the church and watched them grow. I gave myself to the care of my family, and allowed them to minister to me. I made it clear that I had found home among those people, and I dedicated myself to the continuing care of those in my charge. Some, frustrated by my endurance, left for other places, no doubt to find other wildernesses. Many others stayed true to the journey and continued on with me. We have yet to reach our destination, but the journey has resumed. For those who stayed, the bonds which were forged between us during that wilderness time have given us a greater sense of resolve and dedication to the implementation of the Gospel in this place.

Now, watching the snow swirling around my door, I think how much kinder winter is than other wildernesses I have known. Still, I long for spring to return when I can once again work the garden which kept me here.

EIGHTEEN
Longing for an Orchard

For a period of time, my wife and I owned an orchard. Located just outside the charming pre-Revolutionary village of Renssalaerville, New York, our ten acre parcel of land was one of a number of subdivisions created from a former farm. Some of the people who bought pieces of the property acquired a magnificent view of the Catskill Mountains, others got valuable road frontages, still others managed level building sites. Jane and I chose the orchard. To be fair, there weren't many viable trees left, just four or five apple trees on the high part of the ground ending abruptly in a steep drop leading to a small valley which, when we purchased the land, sported a large mirror like pond. We assumed the pond had always been there, but immediately after we bought the property, our heads swimming with thoughts of quiet evenings by the water, the beaver that created the pond moved on, the dam eroded, and four acres of soggy bottom land were left in its place.

Once we had the mortgage, we didn't have the money to build the small geodesic dome we had dreamed of, but we did visit the land and camp on it two or three times a year. Evidence of wildlife was abundant, the changing seasons were spectacular, and it appeared as though the other owners were in the same financial condition that we were since no construction took place for more than five years after our purchase. My wife loved the rolling land and nearby mountains, no doubt reminding her of the dramatic landscapes of her native Lake District in England's north. My daughters loved the cool summer nights and warm days, frequently spent paddling in a nearby *bona fide* lake. I loved the apples.

Our early autumn visit was always my favorite, not just for the incredible display of foliage in a full complement of riotous colors, but also because it was the time when I knew there would be apples. Unlike the carefully pruned and tended apple trees which grew in neat rows in the orchards we passed on our drive to the land, my apple trees were rangy and wild, having been left to grow at will in any direction. Their habit was defined by neglect, having set branches designed for seeking out sun and not for the convenience of pickers. As they had not been sprayed for pests or a variety of fruit tree ailments, much of the fruit was bad—rotted, dwarfed, or inhabited by little creatures who were no doubt glad that the trees had been neglected.

But there was always a handful or bagful of apples that were keepers, looking much as their forebears had when the trees were young and tended by caring hands. We scoured the trees at each autumn visit, fighting the bugs, looking for the best fruit, placing it gently in canvas tote bags. At the end of a morning's picking, we would count our harvest—thirty apples, perhaps forty-five. The children would then run off to the blackberry bushes that protected an old stone drywall and return scratched but delighted that they had found a quart or two of berries. There was always an hour or so of anxious waiting to see if the apple and blackberry pie would emerge intact from the old camp oven. Whether it did or not, it was eaten with pleasure and a fair amount of mess.

I had never seen or tasted apples quite like them. Small and oblong, much like a baseball that has been stepped on by a giant, they were a light shade of yellow green with a blush of pink and red on one side. The flesh was firm, giving a satisfying crunch at the bite, with a tangy, almost tart flavor. The core was wide at the center and narrow but pithy at the ends, shaped much like a child's construction paper lantern. The skin was surprisingly thick. Best of all, they bore little or no resemblance to the items sold in stores which are labeled "apples."

I've never found a supermarket which carries more than five or six kinds of apples—Granny Smith, Red Delicious, Golden Delicious, McIntosh, and (for the adventurous) the occasional Winesap or Cortland. Unfortunately, these are but shadows of fruit. They look something like real apples, but their waxed and labeled outer skin open to a mealy, flavorless inside. They do have an advantage, however, over the apples in my orchard. They are uniform in size and shape, they are easy to pack, and thus, are cheap to market.

I am told that there are more than 7,000 varieties of apple in the world, and that in the eighteenth and nineteenth centuries, more than 3,000 varieties of apple grew in the United States with exotic names like Magnum Bonum, Pound Sweet, Terry Winter and Grimes Golden. Many of these rare varieties are currently collected and grown by individuals who have a passion for preserving uniquely flavorful fruit.

I have no idea what name the apples in my orchard carry. I have taken them into the nearby village and asked a few locals, one of whom responded simply, "Well, it's an apple. You can cook it or eat it." We always take a few home, and I have shown them to those who plant and till, but no one is sure what they might be.

In time, my family moved to a community where even occasional visits to the land were decidedly impractical. After a great deal of hand and soul wringing, we placed the property on the market and it sold within seven months. My only regret was leaving the orchard behind. For years I tried to grow the seed in anticipation of such a move, but without success. It was only after we sold the property that I discovered I should have taken cuttings and grafted them into trunk stock.

Now I stand in a garden comprised primarily of annuals. Everything comes and goes within a single season. When winter ends, everything must begin again. There are, of course, a few exceptions. My asparagus comes back year after year, as does my rhubarb. There are perennials around the house which arrive every year like old friends—astilbe, bleeding heart, columbine—but if they are not supplemented with annuals the house is not supported with color past their blooming cycle. I wish there was something more permanent in my garden that would provide not only for me, but for those who come after me.

The Bible knows about love of orchards. In the Hebrew scriptures, the word for orchard is *pardes*, and while the fruit of ancient orchards was more likely to be pomegranates and olives than apples, I'm certain that all of the elements of orchard tending were the same then as now. But the Bible has a slightly different spin on orchards than we do. *Pardes* was actually a word that was imported into the Hebrew language, in much the same way that we have incorporated words such as hors d'oeuvre or encore into our language. The word originally came from ancient Persia, where it referred to a place of productive planting. The Persian form of the word was paradise. Paradise is the place of the productive planting of God, both on earth and in that place where there is no death, but life everlasting.

I am certain that the apples in my orchard were planted for the planter's particular taste, a particular climate, considering the particular qualities of the soil in which it was planted, but those days are passed and their value is determined not by their uniformity or marketability, but simply because of my pride of ownership and my delight in their uniqueness. If I were to take a basketful to a friends or neighbors, they would no doubt look at the bumps and blemishes on the apples' unvarnished skin, thank me politely, and throw them away.

Ours is an "orchard faith." That is, we who are committed to the mission and fellowship of the church receive something which was planted many years before us. We still enjoy the fruit of those plantings today. Much of what has been planted in the past is of inestimable value and worth tending and preserving for future generations, but, surprisingly, those venerable trees are fewer than we might think. Like an orchard run amuck, the essential fruit of the planting has often been overtaken by cultural practice through the years, like an apple tree that is being choked by a wild vine. In their time, those cultural practices and beliefs may have enlightened those who came to the orchard looking for nourishment. They may have protected the orchard from the encroachment of more aggressive thought and practice. They may have even served to adorn the orchard by adding beauty and dignity in the worship and service of God.

Unfortunately, many of those cultural vines no longer serve their original purpose in a church struggling to minister effectively in the latter half of the twentieth century. In fact, some of them may prevent us from getting near to the heart of the orchard itself and feasting on its bounty. As a result, like my orchard in the Catskills, the church appears to many to be simply a grove of old trees, barely productive, encrusted with practice and habit which makes us look abandoned, untended. The good news is that life still swells in old trees, waiting patiently for the vine dresser to release that which is present and still perfect within. How shall we determine what trees must stay and what growth must be removed?

I am sitting at a conference table in the activity room of a local church, joined by colleagues of other denominations for a monthly meeting of area clergy. We have been talking about our various judicatories' policies on ordination. I express the hope that my own denomination will soon expand the offices of deacon, priest, and bishop to the widest possible range of people. I explain that my belief is that God manifests Godself in every individual, and that as the second century apologist Justin Martyr argued, "the seeds of God" exist in all of us.

"Don't you believe in the Bible, son?" The square jawed minister of a local non-aligned congregation squared off against me, leveled a piercing stare at me that convinced me he was ready for a fight.

Flippancy always adds to a good fight. "Thank you for the compliment," I said. "The closer I get to 50, the less I am called 'son'!" He is not amused. "Of course I believe in the Bible," I say with a new found earnestness in my voice. "As a matter of fact, I have one right here." Reaching into my briefcase, I pull out my favorite pocket-sized edition, feeling as righteous and emphatic as William Jennings Bryan at the Scopes' trial. "How can I deny it's existence when I am holding it in my hand?" Steaming, he clenches his hands together. "You know what I mean. Do you or don't you believe the Bible is the inspired word of God?"

Now we are at it in earnest. "I believe in the God to which scripture consistently points. I believe that the inspiration of scripture can be demonstrated clearly and simply through the realization that despite the discrepancies, despite the mistakes, despite the cultural overtones, the Bible still points unswervingly and unalterably to God."

He is like a James Bond martini—shaken, but not stirred. "Are you aware of what the Apostle Paul has to say about homosexuality? Are you familiar with his teaching that women should not be permitted to exercise authority over men?" I wondered if he had discussed this thorny problem with his wife.

"Are you aware," I asked, "that the Psalmist prays to have his enemies' children bashed against the rocks? Are you aware that the first five books of the Bible sanction polygamy? And this Paul of yours—did you know that he advocated slavery, and urged a runaway slave to return to his master?"

The chairman of the meeting intervened, anxiously urging us to return to the agenda. At least I knew where I *wouldn't* be asked to preach in this year's pulpit exchange.

The Bible, both Old and New Testaments, with all its flaws and imperfections, is still the source book of Christian life. Like maps, some simple and rudimentary, others detailed and clear, each book of the Bible points to the hunger of God to be engaged fully in the human heart. The remarkable thing about scripture is that this clear and direct road sign toward holy living has stood the test of two millennia of study and application. Like a mighty tree which never fails to provide fruit, the Bible is the defining document of life engaging faith. For centuries, it has been mocked, ridiculed, burned, torn apart, analyzed, demythologized, and deconstructed, but its contents still have power to bring men and women to faith, and thus, to grace. This, certainly, must stay in the orchard. However, the vines of inerrancy, absolutism, iconoclasm must depart, for they threaten to obscure our approach to that sign which would lead us to God. Worse, they tempt the spiritually diminutive to brandish it as a weapon, rather than a source of growth and implement of change.

"There's entirely too much laughing in the service!" A member of my congregation stood at the back of the church where I was shaking hands, making sure that his comment was heard by the largest possible audience. I stopped in mid-shake and looked at him. "There's nothing funny about the Gospel. I don't come here to be entertained, I come here to be enlightened. Let's cut the hilarity and get serious about our religion!" He stormed off, leaving me to salvage my morning greetings with something approaching grace. When I had greeted the last person in line, I went to my office and called the man, asking if I could drop by and hear him out more fully. "I don't want to talk to you about it. I just want you to stop all the funny comments in your sermons and in the announcements." That's when I made a fatal mistake. "You know, Joe, I'm sure there are plenty of churches out there where there's nothing to laugh about." I never saw him again.

One of the trees that grows in the orchard of God is the expressive tree of worship. Throughout history, people have gathered to engage in common worship. The forms and rituals they use speak uniquely to them, and may not have relevance or meaning to others who are just as devout, just as fervent in their adoration of God. These ritual forms span the spectrum of human behavior from frenzied dancing to absolute silence. It is the responsibility of each Christian to seek out worship which strikes a chord in their own spirit and allows them to offer themselves without impediment to the holy God. Not every church is good for everybody, and some are good only for a few. However, in our variety of liturgical forms we become something glorious—a kaleidoscope of form and content which is expressive of the tremendous diversity of God. This tree must stay.

A church that thrives on insularity and self-appeasement is as useless as a factory that has no product. It may be a model of efficiency with very happy employees, but unless it has something to contribute to the marketplace, it is worthless. In the same way, churches that exist only to serve their members do not understand Christ. The essence of the Gospel is not self-satisfaction or the production of good feelings about ourselves or others. The Gospel calls us to a radical life of joyful sacrifice for the world. The poor, the sick, the orphaned and widowed, the disadvantaged: these share a special solidarity with God and we who take up Christ's cross embrace them not only as our stock in trade, but as our precious inheritance. The church that is not continually spending itself is being choked by vines of selfishness. Those vines must be torn out by the roots so that the mission of the Gospel may be fulfilled. This tree must stay.

The work of informed inquiry is a vital component of Gospel living. While the canon of Scripture was set early in the church's life, the experience of God with humans continues. The last two thousand years have seen men and women of faith struggling to understand their experience of God, and to frame that understanding in language which allows others to hear and know what God does among people. Some have speculated on the nature and activity of God in ways that have left mainstream Christians uneasy or disturbed. That does not necessarily diminish the importance of the work done by people of faith who have been more adventuresome in their thinking. In the past, those who have embarked on uncharted theological grounds have been labeled heretics, but ours is an age which demands that every voice be heard in the unending quest for divine truth. Further, we must nurture a spirit of inclusivity which provides fertile ground for those who will exercise our relational and spiritual muscle lest we fall into comfortable and predictable patterns of believing, as our knowledge of God is far from reaching the point of exhaustion. Much of the thought produced may be of little or no value, but there will be some thrilling finds as well, in the same way that Zacchaeus was found in the sycamore tree and being found, crafted a Christ-like home. Absolutism of any kind, even draped in the most pious garb, must go. Theological and spiritual inquiry—this tree must stay.

Some would argue that sacraments must stay, or certain orders of ordained ministry, or traditional creedal statements. In that they continue to be expressive of the faith which is in us, and that they provide a medium where we can continue to engage the holy God productively, I would agree. However, we are not wed to these things. I have known people who have languished in prison for many years without benefit of clergy or sacrament who yet maintained a vital and fruitful faith. Their own believing may not have fulfilled the expectations of the Nicene Creed, but they nonetheless endured their imprisonment certain that they were kept company by the One who sustains and abides.

There are certainly a number of vines which must be unearthed from our pleasant planting if the orchard is to thrive. The church has long imposed a system of exclusivity upon people in hopes that such a posture would keep the faithful close to the activity of the church. In the past, ours has been an "ark theology"—that is, if you are aboard this ship, you are saved; if you are not within the protection of the church, you are lost. While it may be true that some people respond well to fear, the plain truth is that the church no longer has the authority in the world to operate a closed system. Even worse, that kind of exclusivity betrays the truth about God. It was my fundamentalist's friend Saint Paul who asserted that the whole creation was saved by the sacrifice of Christ on the cross, and I have come to see and believe that saint and sinner alike are embraced by the grace of God. A Christianity which consigns the profligate to a hell of eternal torment has no room for me, for I, too, am a sinner; a sinner saved, not by my righteousness or my strengths or my personality, or even my believing, but only by the grace of God. Any work or belief which divides the human family into the saved and the damned must go.

There is a fair amount of popular exploration into questions of spirituality today. Many of them are helpful, especially those which seek to translate spiritual experience from the riches of other faith traditions. But other avenues insist that the purpose of spiritual work is to engorge the individual soul, seeking comfort and soothing acceptance of what we already are, without demanding that we become more than we thought we could be. This is not spirituality, it is self-centeredness, and must be rooted out and destroyed.

Magic has always been popular in the church, from investing the clergy with a special (and different) spirituality than the laity to praying for good weather for Saturday's family picnic. It may be ridiculous to think that people ask God to change the world for their convenience, but we do it nonetheless. This is a stultifying and venomous vine that can transform, not only the appearance, but the quality of the fruit available in the orchard. The church, which for so many years gave tacit assent to the propagation of magic within its sanctuaries, must now renounce and repel any suggestion that the creation can be manipulated by supernatural intervention. We must instead learn the true meaning of prayer—that in praying we come into God's presence, and our first task is not to present God with a list of demands, but rather to allow us to be shaped and molded by the demands God has of us.

The work of planting orchards is not accomplished once for all. The orchard of God must be nurtured, pruned and cultivated to provide fruit. Old trees, once fruitful in their time but now exhausted, must be cut down and new trees must be planted in their place. And we will not be surprised when the generations who come after us continue to find fruit still worth picking and strive to keep the planting alive.

NINETEEN

In the Shadow of the Dragon

At one point in my life I wanted to see with my own eyes all of the 103 Messier objects in the night sky—nebulae, star clusters, galaxies and the like that were identified and described by Charles Messier and Pierre Méchain in 1784. These two stellar explorers weren't looking for such things. They simply wanted to eliminate them as possibilities in their search for comets. There is, they thought, nothing quite so annoying as thinking you have found a comet, only to be staring at a gaseous anomaly.

Some people collect stamps, others coins or Impressionist art. I was prepared to collect the Messier objects. With a small telescope mounted on my back deck and a star chart in my hands, I spent many lonely winter nights fighting the cold looking for these starry wonders. It never occurred to me that Messier and Méchain were not hindered by the light pollution which plagues modern night skies, nor that they probably did their looking in an open field and not in my backyard where stately oaks obscured fully one-third of the southern horizon and the back of my house blocked the view to the north. Being unwilling to seek out a large field in the urban sprawl of the New York metropolitan area with rest facilities handy, I was left with a small circle of exploration in the heavens and the hope that sooner or later all of these objects would rotate through my window of opportunity.

After months of bone-chilling searching, I had found three of the objects, two of which can be seen by any school child—the Andromeda Galaxy and the Horsehead Nebula in Orion—and one slightly less obvious— the planetary Ring Nebula in Lyra. Eventually, the sounds of happy children playing inside by the fire seduced me away from my collection and inside to the comfort and warmth of hearth and home. I sold the telescope the following summer and contented myself with the knowledge that I had, in my short astronomical career, seen a small handful of true wonders.

Now I stand in the middle of my garden in the darkened hours of a summer night and realize that in my stargazing days I picked up more than

I realized. I can name the constellations above me which move through the umbrella of the night sky and the major stars which define their ancient forms. Like mobile sentinels, they soar across the heavens nightly inviting me to a daily celebration of their celestial dance. During the growing season, my garden lies in the shadow of Draco the dragon, a large constellation with a dwarf elliptical galaxy as its most prominent feature. Tracing its outline with my eye, I see that it extends from one end of my garden to a point beyond my planting's furthest boundary. Head upturned, I feel the breeze brush the velvety leaves of bird bottle gourds across my legs, hear the sound of crickets and cicadas and swell with excitement that I am part of creation. Still, there's something about that dragon.

This dragon is not the first I have come across. I have spent much of my life in the company of five dragons: self-doubt, egocentrism, mediocrity, decisiveness, and overconfidence. These dragons have been more Chinese than English. That is, while English dragons are always perceived to be evil, Chinese dragons bestow both blessings and curses. So it is with the dragons which have attended my journey. There have been times when their presence and activity has been minimal, other times when they have ascended to prominence in the daily function of my life. They have caused me shame and embarrassment, they are the authors of what little celebrity I have enjoyed. I have learned to view my scaly companions with some detachment, and I work to examine them daily to acquire a more objective analysis of them in themselves and them in me. In doing so, I am unable to avoid a closer look at the soft underbelly of my own emotional and behavioral makeup, expansive and vulnerable. Hence, I continue this process with some anxiety, fearing, at the last, that the dragon may well be me.

In the same way that the stars in the galaxy of Draco can be examined, classified, and cataloged, the behaviors which plague and bless my spirit can be challenged, confronted. Doing so requires the courage of Saint George, for the quest involves the rooting out and destruction (or at least alteration) of that which I have allowed to become an essential part of who and what I am.

My self-doubt is rooted in a belief of my unworthiness to be an effective servant of Christ. I read through the litany of insufficiency that so many of us know by heart. My sins are greater than my goodness, my anger overwhelms my desire for compassion, my need for love and approval often outweighs my desire for righteousness.

I share my egocentrism, my love for self and that which the self demands, with many other people, but take no delight in their company. In fact, the me-insistence of my self-absorption draws my attention away from anyone else in my shallow attempts to satisfy my will.

My mediocrity is apparent when I long to be just another believing Christian—someone who is convinced in the head that there is a God, but hopes that my God will not demand anything particularly taxing from my heart and hands.

Decisiveness seems like a good thing to have, leaving the bearer free of the muddle of too many choices and no clear vision. But as soon as it is born in the human heart, decisiveness quickly mutates into judgementalism—the insistence that the best criteria for assessing worth and value reside in my eye and mind alone. Coupled with rigidity, decisiveness becomes merely a sorting device, sifting people into categories marked "good" and "bad," tasks into "do-able" and "impossible," events into "enjoyable" and "worthless."

Overconfidence is not the opposite of self-doubt, but is rather complimentary to it. My overconfidence asserts that I am complete and whole within myself and require little or no input from others. This last dragon is the most dangerous of all, as properly fed and nurtured, it leads to relational death.

As painful as it is to name these dragons and admit their power over me, it is positively disastrous to allow them to continue to feed on my spirit uninterrupted. They are, I believe, as malignant as any cancer which threatens the vitality of the human body, and uncomfortable as the process may be, I must work to excise them from the garden of God which I struggle to maintain in my soul.

I shift my gaze from the stars above my head to the space around me and see that the fireflies have come out to illuminate my garden. These gentle little lives appear in abundance this year because of an unusually wet spring season. There are so many that the stars seem lost for a moment, my eye drawn to God's pyrotechnic skills.

Now I am surrounded by lights—the lights of the sky and the lights of the garden. Draco, still present, no longer dominates my view because of the golden twinkling around me. Other constellations become readily identifiable—Lyra with her brilliant star Vega, Hercules, graceful Cygnus with shining Deneb at its head, W-shaped Cassiopeia. These, too, are in the heavens and run the night sky just as clearly as the dragon.

I am convinced that one of the greatest curses let loose on human life is *aloneness*. The best and strongest among us have demonstrated our ability to overcome tragedy and disability, but aloneness is a dragon which has no satisfaction in anything other than its complete destruction. We confront aloneness on two levels.

First, there is the experience of being alone in the world, estranged from other women and men in a state of relational separation. In this state we are strangled by our solitude, having no other resource to draw upon than what we carry inside to manage the exigencies of life. Most of the work we attempt in times of aloneness is of little value, for while it may satisfy our own need for expressiveness, it rarely provides others with the intellectual or emotional bridges which allow them to enter our pain. Aloneness shackles the human heart, and its hallmarks are cynicism, bitterness and despair.

But more tragically, there is an aloneness in which we find ourselves divorced from God, left to drift on the boundaries between marginal living and life abundant, never seeing or knowing that measure of divine grace and compassion which certifies our position as loved and cherished by anything beyond ourselves. If aloneness on the human plane is stultifying, aloneness on the celestial plane is deadly. To be separated from God is to be separated from life itself, casting us into a morass of anguish. The Psalmist complains,

> As with a deadly wound in my body,
> my adversaries taunt me,
> while they say to me continually,
> "Where is your God?"

Very often, our aloneness, both terrestrial and celestial, comes from the way we position ourselves in life. Standing alone in the garden, it is not surprising that all I can see is my own insufficiency, my own selfishness. In fact, my realization of the value of the lights above me and the lights around me is more an act of grace than invention, but it is a grace which comes to me because I have placed myself in another arena in other times.

The church, I believe, is the only human institution which places its people in a world with two kinds of light, each demanding the abolition of aloneness. The Christian enjoys the company of those shining souls who are beyond this plane, like the stars in the sky, yet is surrounded by the regular illumination of souls present to us, like the fireflies which twinkle around me.

Like the stars in the night sky, the life and work of those who have gone before me in faith draw attention, not only to my dragons, but to solutions for my despair and inadequacy. However, unlike the stars, they are neither remote nor fixed. In fact, they are interactive companions on the journey. In the liturgy that I have come to love, we proclaim that we are *together* with angels and archangels, with the company of saints and the host of heaven in pointing our gaze toward God and acknowledging God's supreme holiness. This isn't simply a well-crafted idea, it is expressive of our common experience as a people. When we gather at the table to share a meal of simple bread and sweet wine, we pass through the portal of our own limitations to a level of engagement with those who stand in God's nearer presence. Surprisingly, we find remarkable people, not just pasty-faced saints, but men and women who struggled their whole lives with dragons just like ours. In that place, the struggle is honored and each individual life is made a victor.

But lest we lose sight of the totality of this endeavor, God has surrounded us with fireflies as well, those struggling souls who share the earth with us who sometimes manage to shine enough to brighten our dark times. For these, too, are the saints of God, not yet perfect, but longing to be refined. Despite all my dragons, "I mean to be one, too."

TWENTY

Starting All Over Again

The garden is the last place I visit as the movers lift the furniture in the moving van. My family has made this house and yard home for thirteen years and each room, each square of soil is filled with the ghosts of memory, both pleasant and painful. The garden has fed my family and the work it demanded has fed my spirit. Happy as I am to be moving to a new home, I must admit to some lingering sadness at leaving this long, rectangular plot of ground. Ironically, the garden has never been in better shape. Thirteen years of mulch and compost and deep tilling has made the soil rich and light. Every trowelful of soil finds two or three fat earthworms. Acidity and alkalinity have been balanced to perfection. Everything I plant grows, as well as a few things I didn't.

I will dig up some of the perennials and take them with me in buckets—yarrow, crocosmia, the red astilbe, my blue and white columbine, a bleeding heart. Others will have to stay—the clematis that spreads across the stockade fence, the roses, the myrtle I brought north from South Carolina. These now help define the property and deserve to stay for the enjoyment of another.

My other garden—the church I am privileged to serve—has been productive as well, so much so that my wife and I have decided to set our roots even deeper. Moving out of the rectory, we have purchased a home of our own in an adjacent community. This gives us a feeling of being settled far greater than when we lived in the church's house. As well, it makes it clear to my congregation that I have found and still find my deepest satisfaction in working and worshiping with them. There are plenty of churches around, but Saint Martin's has become my family, my spiritual home and I can think of no greater joy than serving this place until I retire.

Some members of my congregation are confused about why I would choose to live in a house of my own rather than the idyllic pastoral setting of the church's campus. "You get your housing for free," they argue, or "You will never find a home as lovely as our rectory."

Well, yes and no. "What would happen if I die?" I ask. "Where would my family live? We have no equity in your house, and you would be forced to ask them to leave." This seems readily understandable to most, and they wish me well in our house hunting. But there is a deeper hunger which I nurse—the desire to live and work in a place of my own, shaping and molding the land to match my dream of what house and garden should be.

The search begins. Our realtor, a member of the congregation, shuttles us from one available house to another. We visit three or four houses a day for a period of three weeks. When we sit down to discuss their merits, Jane and I get them all confused, not entirely certain which family room belonged to which handyman special. We also realize in our visiting that we have different ideas about what the perfect house should be. Jane looks at the kitchen and the amount of light coming in the windows. I look at the yard, including any evidence that a gardener had been here in the past, and for some kind of subterranean space that no one else would want but I could claim as a shop.

Spotting a large, dry, paneled basement area, I would proclaim, "This one looks good to me!" only to have my wife reply, "All the windows would have to be replaced. All of them. Right away." A sunny backyard with turned over tomato cages and bamboo stalks still upright, the remnants of engagement with the soil, prompt me to venture some word of approval. "The foundation's cracked and it needs a new roof," she says. Finally, I get smart. "Why don't you single out a few houses that you are comfortable considering and I'll visit those!" She looks deeply wounded. "I thought we were doing this together," she says. Not so smart after all. We both come to realize that no house is perfect, nor will any house meet all of our expectations, but after three or four weeks of rummaging through the detritus of other peoples' lives, we are ready to resign ourselves to a house, *any* house, that met five percent of our criteria. If the truth were told, even that was negotiable.

Then our realtor friend called. "I have a house you have to see." An exhalation of air resembling a groan arose from the depths of my being.

One walk through the property piqued our interest. In addition to a moderately sized house with enough bedrooms for our daughters, there was a yard which measured a little less than an acre, studded with lilac, hickory, black walnut, cedar, blue spruce, and white oak. Even better, there was a large and sunny open space in the center of the backyard that screamed, "Plant me!" The property was bordered on two sides by streams wide enough and deep enough for trout. We looked at each other and knew—this was home.

The Bible, as much as anything, is the story of people moving on. Adam and Eve are forced to leave the comfort of Eden. Noah is borne by the waters of the flood to a new land. Abraham is called to leave Ur of the Chaldees and find a place that God has appointed for him. Jacob's family migrates to Egypt to escape a famine. Their descendants flee that same land to escape slavery. Israel is carried off in bondage to exile. Forty years later, the prisoners are released by Cyrus and are told to return home. Jesus is born in the midst of a move. Shortly after, his family must move south for protection. When the political climate becomes less threatening, the little family moves to the north of Palestine. In his adult ministry, Jesus must move from the community in which he was raised because he is too familiar to his neighbors. At one point, he says to his friend Peter, "They will take you where you do not want to go." Following Jesus' death and resurrection, the apostles move out to evangelize the nations, having been ordered by the Master, "Go into all the world." Saint Paul moves from continent to continent so often that he has to ask a helper to bring his library and winter clothing to him. The focal point of the fledgling church moves from Jerusalem, where Christians are dying, to Rome, where they are about to die. From beginning to end, the Bible is about moving.

Now, moving, I rehearse its stories looking for confidence and assistance in moving well. "Go from your country and your kindred to the land that I will show you," God instructs Abram. "Let this day be a holy day for you," Moses tells a nation perched on the brink of freedom. "Pray for the welfare of the place where I have sent you," God says to Jeremiah. "When you enter a town," Jesus instructs the wandering seventy, say 'Peace be to you.'" Knowing that no home is forever, the Acts of the Apostles says of Philip, "and passing through, he preached the gospel." These are the marks of moving well.

Unfortunately, the Bible says nothing about cardboard boxes, at least not that I can find. Our move was preceded by four weeks of packing and followed by six weeks of unpacking. While nothing was broken, there was certainly a lot that was disrupted. It seemed that we would never fit into our new home. My wife arranged and rearranged the closets in search of more space, my daughters seemed perfectly content to leave their clothes in boxes and just dip in when they needed something that had been packed. I stood in the yard.

We moved into our home in mid-April which meant that any preparation and planning I was going to do to make a garden space had to be done quickly. Planting time for early crops had almost passed, and I should be ready to set out seedlings by mid-May. All that stood before me was a large circle of lawn. "Just think, honey," my wife said as she came up behind me, "you will be able to create the garden you have always wanted."

The garden I have always wanted. It took me a few minutes to frame a response. "I am already in the garden I always wanted," I said. "In the flower of my family, the fruit of my work, the increasing abundance in my spirit—these are the garden spaces I have always wanted."

Then, I started to dig.